THE BOOK

October 2012 to October 2013

APERIODICAL LLC · SEATTLE, WASHINGTON · 2014

OUR PATRONS

*This book was made possible through the generous support of 1,467
Kickstarter backers who wanted us to make something new and cool. We would like
to thank particularly those supporters who contributed at the patron levels:*

A Kind Anonymous Supporter
A C Black
Adam and Tonya Engst,
  TidBITS Publishing Inc.
Andreas Lehnert
Bill O'Donnell
Brian J. Geiger
Chris Higgins
Chris Krupiarz
Dana Bishop

Derek Groothuis
Doug Park
Ell Neal
Etienne Vlok
First Choice Books
Gail and Kent Higgins
Graham and Joyce Orndorff
Jean MacDonald
Joshua Jones
Leander Kahney
Michael Gartenberg

Philip Borenstein
Pixate, Inc.
Rene Ritchie
Rob Millis
Ryan J. Gilmer
Saul Hymes
TJ Luoma
Toby Malina and Jim Heid
Tom Bridge
Viktor Balogh

THE MAGAZINE

EDITOR & PUBLISHER
Glenn Fleishman

MANAGING EDITOR
Brittany Shoot

COPYEDITING AND PROOFREADING
Scout Festa

BOOK DESIGN
Jessica Simmons,
Rand Ardell, and Chris Moore;
Simmons Ardell Design

WEB DESIGN
Alli Dryer and Jenni Leder;
MEGABRAIN

WEB IMPLEMENTATION
Chris Suave

APP DESIGN
Brad Ellis, Jessie Char, and
Louie Mantia; Pacific Helm

APP DEVELOPMENT
Chris Parrish & Guy English;
Aged & Distilled

JILL OF ALL TRADES
Christa Mrgan

FOUNDER & EMERITUS ADVISER
Marco Arment

Published by Aperiodical LLC,
1904 E. McGraw St., Seattle, WA 98112

http://the-magazine.com/
editor@the-magazine.com

The Magazine is a publication of Aperiodical LLC.
iPhone, iPad, and iPod touch are trademarks of
Apple Inc., registered in the U.S. and other countries.
App Store is a service mark of Apple Inc. All other
trademarks are the property of their respective owners.

Printed in the United States of America.
First edition. First printing, 2014.

978-0-9914399-0-4 – *The Magazine:
The Book* (hardcover edition)

978-0-9914399-1-1 – *The Magazine:
The Book* (electronic edition)

MIX
Paper from
responsible sources
FSC www.fsc.org   FSC® C002589

10 9 8 7 6 5 4 3 2 1

The *Magazine*'s name was always intended as a bit of a joke. The name was a play on Apple's Newsstand: we were *The Magazine* for *The Newsstand*. It was an attempt to make it clear that a new publication designed from the ground up to be a crisp and easy-to-read app for the iPhone and iPad, and which omitted ads and was supported fully by subscribers' fees, wasn't taking itself too seriously. And it stuck.

In defiance of our generic moniker, we set out to deliver a set of specifically interesting stories every two weeks that told readers about topics, people, and places they didn't routinely encounter.

The thread that runs through all of our stories is the strong connection between technology and culture. We sometimes write directly about the electronic realm, such as the game *Journey* ("Strange Game," page 77), a video game that doesn't fit our expectations about what multiplayer Internet interaction is like.

But we also like to find tales that deal with non-digital things. We write about letterpress ("Wood Stock," page 172, and, in the ebook, "Inkheart") and dealing with superannuated chickens ("Laid Out," page 123), cosplay ("Redshirts in the Coffeeshop," page 37) and real play: *Star Trek* performed al fresco in Portland, Oregon ("Boldly Gone," page 21).

In our first 12 months, October 2012 to October 2013, we published over 130 such long-form non-fiction feature stories, some reported and some derived from personal experience. But we were solely a thing in the digital ether — and we wanted to take the most compelling, funny, and offbeat stories from our first year and make them "real." Thanks to the support of Kickstarter backers, this book exists! (If you backed our campaign, thank you for your advance support; if you bought the book later, thank you for enjoying what you found.)

The writers, editors, and artists who contribute and produce *The Magazine* find wonder in the world and in other people, and joy in the collaboration that made this book possible. We're delighted to share some of that with you in our first collection.

Glenn Fleishman
Editor & Publisher
February 9, 2014

BKZ

CONTENTS

A BEACON OF HOPE

By JOHN PATRICK PULLEN

A dying city glows with optimism over its plan for a giant lava lamp.

The nighttime view from Brent Blake's window offers a view straight through downtown Soap Lake, Washington, past the soft glow of the Masquers Theater marquee and the neon beer signs in the Del Red Pub, and ending about a mile away, where paved roads give way to sagebrush, high desert, and darkness. Situated at the corner of Main Street and Highway 17, which sports the town's only stoplight, this view is all most people ever see of Soap Lake, as they blow through headed for anywhere else.

The locals, however — all 1,514 of them — see much more. They see the allure of a rugged, almost Martian landscape carved by the cataclysmal force of an Ice Age flood.[1] They see the potential of a once-bustling wellness-centric resort

Dry Falls above Soap Lake

Appeared in
Issue 21,
July 18, 2013

town about 180 miles southeast of Seattle, where thousands of early-20th-century vacationers spent summers soaking in the lake's magical, healing waters. They see a home base from which hikers, hunters, and boaters have easy access to the outdoors.

And they see hope in a giant lava lamp standing in the middle of town, drawing curious passersby off the highway with a slow, hypnotic, goopy glow.

However, 11 years into efforts to build the 60-foot-tall whimsical wonder, they've also seen the reasons no one has ever before constructed a six-story tower of lights, hot wax, and oil. Impractical, expensive, underfunded, and perhaps even technologically impossible, the Soap Lake Lava Lamp has proved more complicated to build than anyone had ever imagined. And as the concept became bigger than the city itself, they had no alternative but to build it. "The lava lamp will happen in Soap Lake," says Wayne Hovde, the city's former mayor. "When? I can't tell you — but it will happen."

This year, coinciding with the 50th anniversary of the iconic lamp's invention, efforts have renewed to finish the infamous unbuilt public art installation. To date, the idea has undergone three different designs and endured two city mayors, and it may soon outlive its 72-year-old creator. Brent Blake was diagnosed with terminal acute myeloid leukemia last September. He was given two months to live.

Meet Soap Blake

Blake first conceived of building the world's largest lava lamp in May 2002, while staring out the window and thinking of ways to convince motorists to pull into town and spend money. "Ever-changing, never the same — it would draw people like crazy," says Blake. "It would make it a great tourist attraction."

And while the concept may sound bizarre, it seems perfectly reasonable in comparison to Blake's full body of work. An architect, magazine publisher, and artist, the longhaired, gray-bearded impresario seems never to have heard the word "can't." A tour of his Soap Lake Art Museum begins with his electric chess set, made of sockets and light bulbs wired entirely by Blake himself. He mummifies everyday objects like tennis rackets and toaster ovens on commis-

Brent Blake and his electric chess set. **Courtesy of Brent Blake**

sion. On a table sits a model of another proposed project, "Soaphenge," that never got off the ground. A full-sized re-creation of Stonehenge using massive concrete bars of soap, Blake thinks this one is totally doable. "It would only cost around $100,000," he says.

Nearby, at Dry Falls — a horseshoe-shaped chasm 20 miles north of Soap Lake that's 10 times the height of Niagara Falls and is believed to have once been the world's largest waterfall — Blake proposed building a self-perpetuating cascade. The National Park Service, however, politely declined. "If a dry falls is interesting," Blake reasons, "a wet falls is spectacular."

"The lava lamp will happen in Soap Lake," says the city's former mayor. "When? I can't tell you — but it will happen."

Yet the lamp concept caught on with townsfolk mostly because of the bizarre way Blake launched the project. Instead of drawing up architectural plans, looking for land, getting financial support, or even asking the city's permission, he created posters, pulled together a Web site, and launched a two-year marketing campaign that made it seem like the lamp was *already* operational.

With Blake's posters in nearly every business and lava lamps adorning the shops, the idea alone generated a buzz that had been absent from Soap Lake for decades. At the Visitors Information Center, tourists descended from as far away as South Korea and Eastern Europe, asking for directions to the lamp. Media outlets from the BBC to the *Los Angeles Times* also flocked to the city. But when they arrived, they found little more than a dozen closed shops on Main Street.

"This went everywhere in the world, and it's a nonexistent project," says Blake. "It's just make-believe; it's a poster and an idea. But because it was so weird, the media fell in love with it."

And though the lamp has been Blake's foremost project over the past decade, he seems barely wistful about the possibility of not seeing it built. That's because for him, the art is in the effort, not in the effect. "People are hesitant to experiment, try, or do — it's a natural hindrance to expression," says Blake when asked about his legacy. "I say push all that into the background, start throwing paint onto the canvas, and not be worried or afraid that it's not going to turn out right."

There's something in the water

However outlandish the idea was, Blake rallied Soap Lake behind the lamp — an amazing feat considering the typical townsperson's demeanor. Genuinely warm and relentlessly enthusiastic, the citizens of Soap Lake are proud of their home's slow pace and relaxing atmosphere. They call the frenetic corridor of business from Seattle to Tacoma "the other side," and they enjoy the city's two bars and three restaurants. "The majority of people here, if they turn on the faucet and water comes out and flush the toilet and it goes away, they're happy," says Hovde.

Yet despite being one of Washington's poorest cities, Soap Lake has completed an impressive array of projects in recent years, proving — it's hoped — that they'll be able to light the lamp. In 2003, volunteers raised funds for and opened a 200-seat, $810,000 state-of-the-art theater in the town center. In 2009, the Soap Lake Garden Club dedicated a $500,000 sculpture titled *Calling the Healing Waters*, which, at 45 feet wide, is the world's largest human-figure sundial.

Locals have also restored the RV park, repaired the visitors center, and landscaped a rough-terrain golf course. As part of an ongoing $1.5 million plan to redevelop Soap Lake's Main Street with new pavement, wider sidewalks, and even LED lighting, the city hall was also remodeled, the city council chambers relocated, and the police station rebuilt.

The lava lamp may seem frivolous compared to these more practical (or at least achievable) projects, but the idea has a foundation of sound economics. For centuries, stretching back to when Native Americans roamed the Pacific Northwest, people have come to Soap Lake to relieve symptoms of arthritis, psoriasis, Buerger's disease, and Raynaud's syndrome by coating themselves with mud and lying in the sun. The lake is four times saltier than the ocean, has as much alkalinity as an oven cleaner, and is one of Earth's most unusual bodies of water. The National Science Foundation funded a study to examine microbes found there, hoping that they could shed some light on Martian life forms. Researchers found a new genus of bacteria.

Despite years of research, there's no clear reason why the lake is such an effective treatment for skin, muscle, and joint conditions. In the early 20th century,

JTP

MTZ

doctors prescribed long stays at Soap Lake's many sanitariums to their patients. Hotels popped up on the hills surrounding the lake. And until World War II, the town was known worldwide as a booming health resort.

But with the advent of sulfa drugs and penicillin in the 1930s, fewer people came looking for a cure. Then, during World War II, personnel from nearby Moses Lake Air Force Base took over the housing, choking out vacationers. Finally, the construction of the interstate highway system in the 1950s swept road-trippers past the small town. Today, more than a million tourists annually drive 50 miles past Soap Lake to the Grand Coulee Dam, where a laser light show projected onto the embankment coaxes visitors to spend the night.

Some still come for the waters, but even they may wind up disappointed. Since the dam was built, reducing inflows, the mineral

In the early 20th century, doctors prescribed long stays at Soap Lake's many sanitariums to their patients.

content of the lake has declined. And the mineral-water pipeline that pumps lake water to the last two hotels that feature it as an amenity is out of date, and had to be shut down to repair cracks in 2012. It failed again in 2013. At this writing, its future is uncertain.

As times became increasingly hard for the city, it became clear that the lamp could light their future. "You need to find what your city has that no place else does, and just market it until the cows come home," says Eileen Beckwith, who runs the Soap Lake for Locals site with her husband, Burr. "There are other communities that have mineral lakes, but nobody has a giant lava lamp."

This poster attracted visitors who thought the lamp had already been constructed. **Courtesy of Brent Blake**

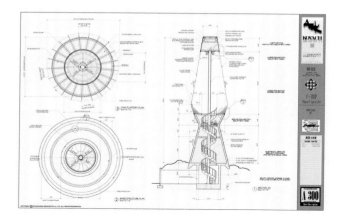

Weird science

As the town embarked on building a 60-foot-tall lava lamp, it quickly became clear why the devices are rarely taller than two feet. In a table-top model, a light bulb heats the mixture of oil and wax inside the lamp. The hotter fluids rise to the top, diffuse heat, and then sink.

To absorb and diffuse heat, a 60-foot lamp would need glass that is 12 inches thick at the base and tapers to four inches at the top — something that has never been manufactured, let alone transported.[2] At that size, the lamp would hold 100,000 gallons of liquid, says Blake, and the precise mixture of oil and wax would depend on the size.[3]

The power required to heat "lava" that size would be immense, not to mention frivolous and environmentally neglectful. And then there are the catastrophic concerns of the disaster that would ensue if the lamp cracked. As the engineering proved to be infeasible, enthusiasm in Soap Lake began to wane. "It looked good on the posters," says Duane Nycz, a member of one of the city's longest-residing families.

And then there's the lamp's association with drugs and hippies, an argument that goes two ways. "[Older] generations that lived through the '70s automatically assume the only people who would want to come are looking to sit in front of it and drop acid and smoke dope," says Burr Beckwith. "They're not aware that there's a whole other generation that doesn't have that broad association with it."[4]

Then in 2004, the town was cursed with a miracle. Target Corp. not only had a 50-foot mechanical iron-and-fiberglass lamp hanging in Times Square, but after a bit of finagling it was also willing to donate the $2 million display to the town and pay the $200,000 to ship it to Washington. The deal seemed too good to be true — and, in many ways, it was.

When the 48,000 pounds of iron and fiberglass were unloaded in Soap Lake, it was clear it had been taken apart to ship without any thought as to how it might be reassembled. No one in town could figure out how to put it back

DZP

Architectural drawings courtesy of Andrew Kovach

together. And the electronic "brain" that controlled the display's lava flow motion was missing. It wasn't freestanding, either; it was designed to be hung, requiring an even larger apparatus.

In order to get the Target lamp to work, the town would have had to ship the pieces back to the Minnesota-based company that originally made the display so they could repair it, create assembly instructions, disassemble it, and send it back to Soap Lake, where it could be built again — all for the bargain-basement price of $600,000. Not only was the cost prohibitive, but the idea of paying it bolstered growing feelings around town that the mechanical solution was kitschy and lackluster. Useless, the Target lamp pieces were tossed, uncovered, into a storage lot a stone's throw from the city's sewage treatment plant.

As the engineering proved to be infeasible, enthusiasm in Soap Lake began to wane.

Meanwhile, in-town bickering over the lamp's placement, funding, and design whittled away support for the project. "To me, it's an idea whose time has come and gone," Nycz says. From the barstools of the Businessmen's Club, a private club that lets guests pay "dues" to enter, to the booths at the B&B Drive-In, where diners still place food orders from cars, many still wanted the lamp, but they wanted the real thing. DNQ

And while time proudly stands still in this community, patience was running out. "How long does an idea live?" asks local filmmaker and lamp-booster Kathy Kiefer. "Ultimately, that is the question."

The lamp in a new light

In late 2010, Soap Lake architect Andrew Kovach came up with an ambitious new plan. The design called for scrapping the Target parts altogether and building an imitation lava lamp from scratch. The plans for the state-of-the-art installation proposed using interior solar-powered laser projectors to shoot lava-flow imagery onto an outer shell made of Tenara fabric. The uncannily authentic-looking lamp would have landscaping that would make it look as if it had just sprouted from the ground, and it promised limited light pollution. Similar in LPK concept to a light-up Santa lawn ornament — only much more sophisticated and serious — it also came with a $1 million price tag.

Kovach drafted full schematics and created a preview video, and as he showed them around town, the buzz came back. Blake immediately backed the plan, the mayor approved it, and people like Kiefer and the Beckwiths became downright giddy. "It's like when you have two shots of whiskey and you feel real good inside," says Burr Beckwith. "That's what happened instantly when I saw it."

But financially, the timing couldn't have been worse. With a 34 percent decline in tax revenue over the past four years, the city has struggled. Infrastructure needs such as problematic sewers pulled Mayor Hovde's attention from the project, and then an election season devoid of lava lamp talk (at the project developers' request) brought in a new administration.

The new mayor, Raymond Gravelle, had been the project manager for the *Calling the Healing Waters* sculpture, which took 13 years to plan, fundraise, and build. He relocated to Soap Lake eight years ago after he and his wife passed through looking for the non-existent lava lamp on a motorcycle tour of the state. With the project in its eleventh year, Gravelle has a surprising time frame to get it built. "We hope to be completed before winter sets in," he says.

One reason why it can progress so quickly is that Kovach has spent the recession clearing the runway. Legal documents have been drafted, the land has been set aside, trademark issues have been sorted through, and architectural plans have been refined. "We've gone through great pains to convince people this is the real deal," says Kovach. "We've got hard-line construction numbers for everything right. We know exactly what it's going to cost."

But they don't know where they will get the money. With a high number of Seattle's tech millionaires based in the area, Kovach thinks the funding could likely come from just a few people. Gravelle, meanwhile, thinks that one corporate sponsor could pay for it all in exchange for naming rights. One name that will be on the lamp, for sure, is Brent Blake's. And though time is running out for the lamp's mastermind, the mayor asked if he would say a few words at the dedication. "Brent immediately responded, 'I'll start writing the dedication speech right now,'" Gravelle says.

Yet true to the tale, it's possible he still hasn't finished. "Even when you're told you've only got a couple of days, you still procrastinate," says Blake. "We can't take care of everything, so we do the best we can." These days, that involves a regimen of antibiotics, dieting, and juicing. And since he's survived six months longer than expected, it's tantalizing to think he could live to be 92 years old, like both his mother and grandmother did, but that's more outlandish than a 60-foot tower of molten wax and oil.

Meanwhile, the town Blake is leaving behind is doing its best to carry on his legacy. The project has clearly become Kovach's charge, but the lamp itself seemingly belongs to everyone and no one at the same time.

"It will draw more attention to the wonders we have around here that a lot of people don't really understand," says Kovach. And in that respect, the Soap Lake Lava Lamp makes perfect sense.

Not everything that occurs in nature can be easily explained. Sometimes soaking in magic water can relieve decades of pain. Somehow a coating of mud can clean up old wounds. Dry falls can be every bit as majestic as roaring rapids, and the most amazing lakes can appear in the middle of rocky, dry terrain.

Then there's that other truth, perhaps the most inexplicable of them all: "The lava lamp will pave every street in town," says Hovde. "Nothing else will do that."

Afterword *Brent Blake passed away September 24, 2013. He did not give a speech at the lamp's dedication, which, as of early 2014, has yet to take place. Meanwhile, a new nonprofit group, Friends of the Lower Grand Coulee, has selected the Soap Lake Lava Lamp as its flagship project. The group has been raising funds, and their first project is to build a trail that leads from Soap Lake's East and West beaches to the lamp's site. A downtown building has also been secured for constructing the lamp's top portion.*

The city's plan is to assemble the lamp piece by piece, as funds are raised. The admission fee for the building will help finance the final installation of the lamp on Soap Lake's shore. No completion date has yet been targeted.

---

1 Soap Lake was formed in the first burst of the Great Missoula Floods, an event that began when the ice dam at Montana's Clark Fork River broke, flooding the Pacific Northwest with a 300-foot-tall wall of water some 14,000 years ago. The lake's basin was carved by the initial impact of the flood, which gradually eroded land 20 miles northwest all the way to Dry Falls, creating a series of other mineral lakes along the way.

2 Blake claims to have contacted all the major glass manufacturers in the world, and says Corning was "just dumbfounded by the concept."

3 According to Blake, the lava mixture is confidential, like the recipe for Coca-Cola, and differs based on the size of the lamp. " To think about the experimenting to make the giant lamp work, it would be endless," he says.

4 Of course, in November 2012, Washington State decriminalized marijuana. So now people actually could, potentially, smoke pot while enjoying the lamp.

Clarion Call

An Alaskan singer goes it alone – with a little help from her fans.

By KELLIE M. WALSH

"Lyrics first, and usually there's kind of a spark that makes the lyrics go. If I have a concrete idea, it's so much easier."

Alaskan singer-songwriter Marian Call sits in the finished basement of the home of a board-game designer in an affluent suburb of New Jersey, describing her creative process.

"Once in a while [a song] will come out fully formed...Other ones are like little puzzles. It reminds me of doing quadratic equations. The quadratic formula is so beautiful and elegant. I loved algebra: there was always an answer. You just had to balance and [go] back and forth until you got the answer. I loved making things balance."

Call munches on a post-concert snack of raw broccoli and a cupcake. She has a tall smile, ghostly skin, and dark shadows beneath her eyes that swear to her diligence and autonomy as an independent artist. "Now it's hard for me to see a song if I don't construe it as like a little problem for myself, a problem to solve. There's something very right-brain about the idea, and there's something very left-brain about the solution."

You could say the same about Call's career.

One listener at a time

Call has no label, no manager, no agent, no day job, no trust fund, and no health insurance. She writes, sings, edits, produces, mixes, arranges, performs, schedules, books, and promotes her music herself.

But describe her career as DIY, and she demurs, insisting that to call her independent as an artist is to miss the interdependence with her audience she requires to sustain herself. "I'm a big fan of this old-fashioned village fiddler model," she says, referring to a system in which the villagers may not pay the musician much, but they make sure he doesn't starve. "There's something about that that works for me."

"I will have made it when I have health insurance and can go to the doctor or dentist when I want to." — CALL

Old-fashioned models applied with new technology are, in fact, the bedrock of Call's career. While many artists feign interest in fan engagement and the disintermediation of art, Call has made them the foundation of her business and her lifestyle. She sleeps on fans' couches; she holds concerts in their living rooms. She lives much of her life on social media. Her home base may be Juneau, but her potential market is the entire Internet.

And through strong vocals, clever songwriting, and a relentless work ethic, Call has built a network of approximately 10,000 fans — included among them Wil Wheaton and the cast of Mythbusters.[1]

But in lieu of mainstream fame, a record deal, or label representation ("No, no, no, I'm deeply uninterested in those things"), she maintains a modest definition of success: "I will have made it when I have health insurance and can go to the doctor or dentist when I want to, and when I am out of debt."[2]

Artist, starving

"Like Amanda Palmer, I'm not afraid to take your money," Call is fond of saying. "But we have a very, very poor relationship in this country between arts and money. We're very, very squeamish about it. We think that there's this purity about arts that we don't want to connect it to money."

 Type http://magcode.me/ plus a blue code in the margin to visit the related Web page.

Call counts her audiences mostly by the dozen and her wages in increments of $10 and $20 through CD sales, digital downloads, and concert donations.[3] Nearly all of her music is available to listen to online for free.

To understand why Call's ability to support herself through music is impressive, consider some better-known contemporaries. Corin Tucker, founding member of the riot grrrl band Sleater-Kinney, works a day job. Cellist Zoë Keating, despite mainstream recognition and 1.2 million Twitter followers, makes just $900 from 232,000 streams of her music; that's less than one-half penny per play. Punk icon Exene Cervenka stopped taking medication for multiple sclerosis because the costs without health insurance were prohibitive.

In a 2011 TEDx talk, Call described how she must convince people "intentionally and repeatedly" to pay for what she calls art's spiritual value. In a landscape in which audiences expect to consume media for free, she explained, "The current market value of my product is zero dollars...I'm basically on an educational mission in order to get paid."

Spiritual value or no, art for a living requires commerce. Raised in a musical family outside Tacoma, Washington, Call recognizes the necessity of good business skills. She may also have picked up a survival trick or two during her classical music studies at Stanford. One such trick: commissions.

Nerdy undertones and overtones

Call credits her career to discovering three things: the tenacious spirit of Alaska, the unmediated connection between artist and audience on MySpace, and the complex relationships of space cowboys on the TV show Firefly.

The three came together in May 2007 when Call, then 25, won a *Firefly*-inspired songwriting contest.[4] With sales of her just-released debut album, *Vanilla*, buoyed by the attention of the Browncoats,[5] Call set off in 2008 on her first-ever tour, traveling through the Western United States and Canada in her home/tourbus, a converted vintage Greyhound dubbed the Millennium Tortoise.

As Jonathan Coulton has proved, the online market, especially for art aligned with geek culture, is a powerful one. Later that year, sci-fi/fantasy collectable makers Quantum Mechanix commissioned Call to write and record a full-length album.

Raised on Joni Mitchell, They Might Be Giants, and Beethoven, Call describes her innate style ("the music that I make when I'm doing it for me") as having "a lot of nerdy undertones and references, but it's a little bit more discreet; it's a little bit more embedded in the identity of it." *Got to Fly* (2008), in contrast, is entrenched in its geek tribute album status, featuring songs inspired by *Firefly* and *Battlestar Galactica* and including Call's popular "I'll Still Be a Geek After Nobody Thinks It's Chic (Nerd Anthem)."

> *"The current market value of my product is zero dollars...I'm basically on an educational mission in order to get paid."* — CALL

Though they sometimes venture outside her natural tendencies, Call says she loves commissions, especially having a concrete idea to wrap her brain around. And the end product is always her own. "Good Morning Moon," a jaunty wake-up call to astronauts, is quintessential Call. It would also be perfect for an Apple commercial.

The mother of invention

"This is the saddest & hardest sort of announcement to make," Call wrote on her blog in March 2009, "but at some point it must be made." Her career had been gaining traction: her first tour broke even, and online sales of *Vanilla* had increased "tenfold." But in early 2009 Call and her husband separated. "I didn't really have a plan," she says. "I was in Seattle; I was in the middle of a tour. I didn't know where to go. I didn't know what to do. I didn't even have a car."

In addition to the emotional impact, the separation had substantial financial repercussions: with her husband remaining in Seattle with the tourbus, Call lost both her financial safety net and her physical home. Now effectively homeless, she had to choose between getting a "real job" and continuing to pursue music.

Just before Kickstarter launched to streamline and popularize crowdfunding, Call invited fans to support her through patronage. Donors' Circle members invest in her art — in her future — in exchange for perks like exclusive tracks and the chance to contribute a voice to her next album. (Singer-songwriters Kristin Hersch and Jill Sobule succeeded using similar models in 2007 and 2008, respectively, and continue to do so.)

Meanwhile, with no home to return to and despite a fear of driving, Call financed her first car and finished what she would later call the "Slow Tour," for its pace and illogical logistics.

The shared experience of this kind of small-scale entertainment creates a bond between Call and her audience.

Fan-powered

Sitting on the sidewalk in Seattle without a plan turned out to be a watershed moment for Call. To maintain forward momentum, she crisscrossed the continent the following spring. Sans promoter, manager, or booking agent, she took the Coulton model of tour scheduling to a new level, mobilizing fans through social media to not only help build the itinerary but, whenever possible, provide overnight accommodations as well.

Across all 50 US states and six Canadian provinces — in backyards and living rooms, on beaches and porches, even in one hair salon (plus wootstock and Comic Con) — Call sang. This tour of primarily house concerts ("house" being loosely defined) provided an intimate setting for Call's acoustic sound and a communal, participatory experience that neither traditional venues nor MP3s can capture.[6]

But touring is expensive, and Call's tours generally make only enough to sustain themselves. ("My food and bills get paid, and I live to fight another month," she says.) The activity increases Internet buzz, however, which increases online sales.

Touring also creates the one-on-one connection crucial to Call's longevity. The shared experience of this kind of small-scale entertainment — of the banter between songs, of sharing a beer together, of providing crash space — creates a bond between Call and her audience. It creates investment and friendship. It also creates future customers.

The album born of these experiences was released in October 2011. A double album, *Something Fierce* reflects an "emotional maturity" that Call says results from the "grown-up things songwriters are supposed to do" that she'd never done. Among them: deciding what to do for a living, being "broke with no recourse," and suffering heartbreak. More grounded than her earlier efforts, Something Fierce displays a confidence that transforms her quirky, sometimes clunky, combination of folk, nerd-pop, and jazz into a soaring, tangly testament to courage, love, home, and her adopted state of Alaska.

Building on this success, Call in the summer of 2012 launched the Marian Call European Adventure Quest, a *Legend of Zelda*–esque Kickstarter campaign complete with 8-bit color graphics. She set a whimsical goal of $11,111 to fund her first European tour and to record a live album along the way. Fans knocked that number down in three hours, and the project grossed $63,000 by its end.

Despite the success, however, Call found herself with higher bills and lower cash in pocket than expected.[7] After fees, taxes, and the cost of the tour, promotion, production, and rewards, she says, "I'm walking away with $8,000 less debt." She estimates that she is living close to minimum wage — yet "that's successful as an artist as defined by many of my friends."

In(ter)dependence

Call is still working to fulfill her Kickstarter campaign rewards more than a year later. She also maintains relationships on social media, and she estimates that she spends 90 percent of her time doing administrative work like emails, logistics, spreadsheets, and mailings. The trade-off of independence requires choosing either concentrating fully on art and giving up control of the business, or running the business and squeezing the art in "around the edges."[8]

Now 31, Call just released the album *Sketchbook*, a barebones production recorded mostly in homes on tour. Her 200-plus days on the road each year don't allow much creative studio time, so she travels with a portable recording rig. "I feel very determined," she says, "and that means that I just do what you have to do where you have to do it."

She laughs, but *Sketchbook* is a good example of the art/money conundrum. The next phase of her artistic cycle, she says, is to stay home to write and record. But doing so requires a sustainable Internet income, which requires products. And products require staying home to write and record.

"Staying ahead of that curve is a constant challenge," Call says. She's intent, however, on spending more time in Juneau making art in 2014. She already has new endeavors in mind and continues to pursue alternative streams of funding.

Fearlessly entrepreneurial and fiercely generous

While describing her artistic cycle, Call interrupts herself in mid-sentence. Wisps of red hair circle her face. "See, thinking this way? All of this thinking this way is why 'fearlessly entrepreneurial' matters to me."

Call is referring to a tweet she'd sent at the Alaska Arts Conference: "Just heard the phrase I want on my epitaph, re. the arts: 'Fearlessly entrepreneurial & fiercely generous.' working toward it. #akartsconf."

"A lot of people are fearfully entrepreneurial, or afraid of being entrepreneurial," she says, "or hate money because it has hurt them so much, like a dog that's bitten them before. Or hate people who make money because they are not making money, and they're upset by this. It's something I deeply understand. I lived for a long time without anywhere to go, staying on people's couches and sleeping in my car and in a tent sometimes. I have fewer illusions about money than I did. But I also think that being afraid of it is not a good solution."

Call uses "entrepreneur" without opportunism; rather, she epitomizes her belief that entrepreneurship and generosity are not antithetical. Upon succeeding at that European Kickstarter campaign, for example, Call immediately made pledges to other Kickstarters.

Perhaps therein lies the balance, the x in the equation of making a living on interdependence. "If I stop being a generous person, or if I'm not a generous enough person, then that would be my definition of failure," Call says. "Money is not worth very much if you don't spread it around to other people."

---

1 Call estimates 10,000 based on mailing list subscribers and social networks.

2 The effect of the Affordable Care Act for Call remains unknown.

3 Call usually requests donations for performances rather than setting ticket prices.

4 The "Sing a Song of Saffron" contest was judged by, among others, actress Christina Hendricks, *Firefly*'s Saffron herself.

5 Browncoats are *Firefly* fans.

6 John Vanderslice described his first experience with house concerts as "intense." QNN Manjula Martin wrote about Vanderslice's Tiny Telephone recording studio in "Flaws and All," in Issue #20 (July 4, 2013). GMJ

7 This situation is not uncommon. Even Kick- ZZR starter says so. Palmer (though not without QGJ controversy) found herself in similar hot water numbers-wise. VGQ

8 Call is not alone in this conundrum. Angela Webber, fellow independent artist and one-half of the Portland-based duo the Doubleclicks, wrote via email, "It's hard to find the balance between doing all of the business and finding new gigs, and trying to make time to actually write songs.... And if you spend all day sending e-mails, you really don't have anything interesting to write songs about."

Boldly Gone

Portland's *Trek in the Park* ends its five-year mission.

By CHRIS HIGGINS

Appeared in
Issue 24,
Aug. 29, 2013

I meet Jesse Graff when he comes to inspect the new heat pump in my Portland, Oregon, bungalow. Graff strings a measuring tape through my house, and we get to talking about life, work, and energy efficiency. As he steps off my porch, he turns back and asks, "Have you heard of *Trek in the Park*?" I reply, "Please come into my kitchen and tell me everything."

Graff explains that by day, he's a tax appraiser for Multnomah County. By night, he portrays Spock in *Trek in the Park*. His mission? Aside from raising my property taxes, he and the crew of the USS *Enterprise* put on eight performances each summer. They drew crowds in the thousands to watch episodes of the original *Star Trek* performed as stage plays in Portland's Cathedral Park.

This August, the five-year mission came to a close as the crew performed the classic *Trek* episode "The Trouble With Tribbles." Opening weekend, on a blistering 95° F Sunday, I joined thousands of devoted fans and watched Graff boldly go where no tax appraiser had gone before.

Taken August 11, 2013, from the St. Johns Bridge above Cathedral Park. **Photo by Mick Orlosky/redfishingboat**

Amok Time

A few weeks before the final run of *Trek* shows, I spoke with Graff and his compatriots: Adam Rosko, who plays Kirk and directs the plays, and his sister, Amy Rosko, who produces them. As we sit down in a local pizza joint, a pair of fans call out from the corner: "Captain Kirk! We're your biggest fans!" Adam smiles and waves — and he does look a bit like William Shatner, even though he doesn't yet have his *Trek*-style haircut, which features pointy sideburns.

Graff, who sports a full Riker-esque beard when it's not show season, says, "I get to spend most of my life incognito. I don't get recognized hardly at all." The only visible evidence that he's Spock is a tattoo of Leonard Nimoy's autograph on his right arm.[1]

Graff asks, "Have you heard of Trek in the Park?" I reply, "Please come into my kitchen and tell me everything."

FJX Adam was just 23 when he and Amy started Atomic Arts, the theater company that staged the *Trek* shows as well as a few other productions in Portland. The siblings searched for an idea that would make compelling outdoor theater and that was not Shakespeare. Going through their DVD collection, they came across *Star Trek*, and it seemed an obvious fit: it had colorful costumes, extended fight scenes, and a built-in fan base.

Adam says, "The first YouTube video [we found] was Kirk and Spock fighting. I thought, *I could see that in the park. That would be hilarious.* Then we watched the whole episode."

That episode was "Amok Time," and it became the first *Trek in the Park* production in July 2009. Adam met Graff in a production of *Robin Hood* ("We were bad guys," Graff recalls); Paul Pistey (their original Bones) was brought onboard shortly after.[2]

The Atomic Arts crew performed the episodes as written, preferring not to add campiness or wink at the audience. Because the show has an element of camp to it already, the material didn't need embellishment. "[We] embrace the silliness. I think that the harder you embrace it, the better reaction you'll get from an audience," Adam says.

In the park

Watching "The Trouble with Tribbles" performed live is an odd delight when you're used to watching *Star Trek* on TV. The audience in the park laughs at the show's many small gags, cheers during the big brawl scene, and hoots as tribbles (fuzzy fur-balls about the size of kittens) pile up onstage throughout the show.

The episode's plot starts with a dispute over a shipment of grain, but is rapidly sidetracked when Lieutenant Uhura receives a pet tribble from a shady trader on a space station. The tribble multiplies, causing an uncontrollable population boom that threatens to overwhelm the *Enterprise*. Bones (played by Jake Street) remarks, "The nearest thing I can figure out is they're born pregnant, which seems to be quite a time saver."

The audience eats it up. Then Bones seals the deal with the classic line, "It seems they're *bisexual*, reproducing at will. And, brother, have they got a lot of will!" He's a doctor, dammit — not a sexologist.

Kirk (Adam Rosko) and Spock (Jesse Graff) discuss the growing tribble problem. **Play photos by Chris Higgins**

Kirk, after opening a tribble-filled hatch

The park setting also mixes super fans with casual fans, *Trek*-loving families, and people who just happen to wander by on a sunny day. On the day I saw "Tribbles," a family settled on the blanket to my left, and a woman struck up a conversation. "My son Ryan is in the play," she says. "He's — I'm not sure which character it is; he does an accent." Another woman, camped out on the blanket in front of us and reading a massive book, turns around. "Ryan Castro? Yeah, he's Chekov," she says. Later, we all share sunscreen.

"It seems they're bisexual, reproducing at will. And, brother, have they got a lot of will!" He's a doctor, dammit — not a sexologist.

Hardcore Trekkies sometimes want the troupe to add material to the show. This year, fans wanted an entire scene from an episode of *Deep Space 9* added to the original "Tribbles"; Adam compromised by adding a few Klingons in the background of the play's closing scene.

The crew's dedication to the original show impressed David Gerrold, author of the original "Tribbles" episode in 1967, who traveled to Portland for a show in August. "The cast was terrific," he writes via email. "Their enthusiasm and playfulness was infectious. They were clearly having a lot of fun reinterpreting the original script, [and] I laughed my ass off. (If anyone finds a flabby old ass somewhere in the park, it's probably mine.)" Gerrold joined the cast onstage after the show; his ass appeared to be intact.

One of the challenges of mounting "Tribbles" was simply getting the tribbles themselves. A year prior to the performance, the crew put out a call for fans to help make the furry props. Bags of homemade tribbles arrived from Alaska, Virginia, and points in between. Portland's Jack London Bar hosted several *Star Trek* craft nights, during which fans made tribbles in an ad hoc assembly line. Costumer Marge Rosko (Adam and Amy's mother) laughs as she describes the end of the process: "They had a girl or two with wire combs brushing them, so all the tribbles had a little 'do when they were done."

Gerrold, who invented the tribble, approves. "They looked like real tribbles to me."

Trailer in the park

Trek in the Park was an immediate hit when it started five years ago, but the crew was prepared for failure. A key decision came at the end of the first performance of "Amok Time" in Woodlawn Park, which happened to be a few blocks from Amy's house. The crew had hastily prepared what they called a "trailer" promoting the next year's show, but they didn't know whether their play would be received well enough to warrant continuing the mission through a second year, let alone its planned five years.

"I opened my mouth, the whistle went off again, and I lost it. I keeled over on the chair. Put my head down in my arms." — GRAFF

As the crew took their bows, they looked to Adam and he said one word: "Trailer." They launched into a two-minute live preview of the next year's show, "Space Seed" (the episode that was the starting point for *Star Trek II: The Wrath of Khan*). From that moment on, *Trek in the Park* was a juggernaut, drawing enormous crowds and forcing the group to relocate to Portland's iconic Cathedral Park, which features a stage and a massive lawn bowl that can accommodate thousands.[3]

The show featured a live band plus sound effects for doors, transporters, and the like. During transporter scenes, the actors stand ramrod-straight as the distinctive sound effect plays, and the audience chuckles. The production was the subject of a doctoral thesis on "geek culture in theater," appeared in a *Portlandia* skit, and became a mainstay of Portland summer fun.

And it remained free the whole time, as local businesses pitched in to donate sets and other help in exchange for appearing in the programs distributed in the park. The cast carefully avoids talk of copyright or legal issues, and I did not ask Paramount (which Graff jokingly calls "Starfleet") for comment, lest the apparently cultivated ignorance at the studio that let it persist was shed.

The show has suffered minor mishaps endemic to any public performance,

though the audience takes them in stride. During the first summer of the show, an earthbound vessel hurtling past the park interrupted Spock's Vulcan mating ritual. Graff recalls, "Spock's having a *pon farr* moment and I'm trying to explain to Kirk why this is happening. I open my mouth and the loudest train whistle I've ever heard goes off. It was like *Inception*. So I stopped, and we wait. Then I open my mouth again, and the whistle goes off again. It's literally the longest train whistle I've ever heard — it went on for 10 or 15 seconds. So we hold it."

Adam interjects, "I could tell you were going to break."

Graff continues, "My mouth was starting to go and I had one more shot. I opened my mouth, the whistle went off again, and I lost it. I keeled over on the chair. Put my head down in my arms. Adam covered. He had the most beautiful cover I've ever seen. He didn't even crack a smile. He just puts his hand on my back, punches an imaginary button, and he says, 'Mr. Spock, keep it steady, will you?' The crowd lost their mind. It was fantastic."[4]

Scotty (Nate Ayling), moments before throwing the first punch in a brawl with Klingon officer Korax (Royal Hebert). Korax incited the fight by saying the Enterprise *"should be hauled away as garbage."*

Generations

Trek in the Park has always been a family affair. Marge Rosko, mother of Adam and Amy, says she made around 50 costumes over the five-year mission. She says "the kids" told her what they needed, and she sewed the outfits at home, sometimes with the help of costumer Benja Barker, who also appeared as an actor in four of the five productions. (In "Tribbles," Barker played Lurry, the man in charge of the Deep Space K-7 station.)

Marge's influence goes deeper than costuming, though; she was the original Trekkie in the family. Marge attended Chicago's first *Star Trek* convention, held at the Conrad Hilton Hotel in 1975. Wandering through the crowd of likeminded fans, she bumped into her cousin. She jokes, "I said, 'Oh, this is too much! Now *family* is involved.' That's always been a joke since then."

As kids, Adam and Amy watched *Star Trek: The Next Generation* with their mother, helping her record the show on VHS tapes. The kids weren't fans in

Curtain call at the final performance of Trek in the Park *on August 25, 2013. Front row, starting at left in red: Al Rosko, Marge Rosko, Amy Rosko, Adam Rosko (Kirk), Jesse Graff (Spock), Ryan Castro (Chekov), Dana Thompson (Uhura), Jake Street (McCoy), Nate Ayling (Scotty)*

those days, though. "It was [my] one program. It was just something to do together," Marge says. Adam says that when *Trek in the Park* started, he was a "very casual" fan, though after five years playing Kirk he has become well-versed in serious fan topics, including the relative merits of *Trek* movies (he says *The Wrath of Khan* is the best).

Graff's friends told him that *Trek in the Park* is their kids' only version of *Star Trek*; they have no concept of Shatner and Pine, or Nimoy and Quinto. He says, "There's one kid who was only a few months old the first year, and [her parents] brought the kid every year. She's going to be four this year." Every year, those parents took a photo with the cast and their daughter, including a bittersweet final photo after "Tribbles."

Marge's influence goes deeper than costuming, though; she was the original Trekkie in the family. Marge attended Chicago's first Star Trek *convention, held at the Conrad Hilton Hotel in 1975.*

The final frontier

Back in the pizza place, the fans approach Adam, asking him about the show. He explains that this year is the last hurrah, the end of the five-year mission. A few beers later, he tells me the ending of the run has gotten him nothing but criticism. "People don't like things that end," he explains.

In the original *Star Trek* series after it made the jump to movies, several of the core crew went off and became captains of their own ships. The *Trek in the Park* crew members are mirroring that, beginning their own next missions. Graff is getting married soon, thinking about having kids, and preparing for his next acting projects. Adam wants to do more personal theater projects and prove that *Trek* isn't his only gig. He's also a production assistant for the TV show *Grimm*, which shoots in Portland.

"It's a big commitment every year; it takes up the majority of your summer. It's great to do something in a town like Portland and have it be appreciated. It makes you feel like you're on the right side of things," says bandleader Peter

Dean. "I'm sorry to see it go. But at the same time, wasn't the last episode of *The Next Generation* called 'All Good Things...'?"

Reflecting on the experience, Adam, Amy, and Graff all liken the final show to a graduation ceremony. "It's scary because I'm dropping the most successful thing that's ever happened to me," Adam says.

Graff says he's looking forward to having his summers free for the first time since 2008. "[My fiancée] Rebecca loves the show. We met through *Trek*. But she's like, 'Honey, I would like to go camping.'"

Afterword *The week after this article was published, Graff and his fiancée, Rebecca, were married. They held a small service in Cathedral Park, near the stage where Trek in the Park had finished its run. Adam Rosko was Graff's best man. Graff also got a job coaching JV2 basketball at Scappoose High School, and he is exploring new acting projects. Adam and Amy Rosko have not yet announced their next project, but Graff suggests it may come in 2015.*

1   He says he's reserving his left arm for Zachary Quinto, who plays Spock in the recent *Star Trek* film franchise reboot. If Quinto isn't available, he says he'll settle for Shatner.

2   Pistey, Graff's former roommate, now lives in South Korea teaching ESL classes. He had to miss the final summer of shows.

3   The original "Tribbles" episode concludes when Scotty explains that he beamed a ship-load of tribbles onto a Klingon vessel — and that's how the *Trek in the Park* version ends too, except we see Klingons drawing swords upstage. This is a deep cross-Trek-series reference. In a time-travel episode of *Deep Space 9* called "Trials and Tribble-ations," Worf informs Odo that tribbles "were once considered mortal enemies of the Klingon Empire," and that "an armada obliterated the tribbles' home world." Odo asks Worf, "Do they still sing songs about the great tribble hunt?" I infer that this Klingon/tribble beef resulted from Scotty's transporter stunt in the original series, plus the fact that tribbles love humans and Vulcans, but hate Klingons.

4   The crew painted the stage gray and tagged its corners "NCC-1701," the original *Enterprise*'s registry number.

5   Graff says that the Portland paper *Willamette Week*, in their annual "Best Of" issue, awarded that moment "Best Unintentional Sexual Innuendo Cameo By An Inanimate Object." I could not find confirmation of this after some research, but it seems logical.

Everyday Superheroes

The mask isn't coming off any time soon.

By SERENITY CALDWELL

F our nights a week, I disappear for hours at a time, leaving Serenity Caldwell behind. She isn't much use where I go. Those I associate with know me only by a pseudonym; I am costumed beyond recognition. I step into a different life as I don new garb and fly down concrete floors. I get beat up. I perform feats Serenity would marvel at. And then I transform back into myself.

The next day, I nurse new and unusual aches in unexpected places. "No," I tell the concerned CVS cashier awkwardly eyeing three finger-shaped marks on my forearm, "I'm not in any trouble at home." But that's all I can say. All I can ever say. Because, really, how do you tell someone that you've become a superhero?

It's not like I planned it this way. Growing up, most kids wish for masks and superpowers. Not me. My kid self would have been delighted to wake up one day and find herself with Jedi powers; I always fancied being the brains rather than the brawn. Not that we ever get what we want.

Have no fear, citizens

It starts quite by accident, with something ever so small: a seed of discontent in

Appeared in
Issue 6,
Dec. 20, 2012

your current activities; boredom; craving something more. And there, in the shadows, your superhero life lurks, just waiting for you to take a turn down that dark alley.

The first meeting doesn't leave an impression. A friend of a friend may be involved, and you agree, after being implored many times, to tag along to something that you think holds no interest. You may see a poster in the square, or spot an article online. It's neat, you think, but nothing more than that. It's only when you reflect on events that you can pinpoint the genesis.

Before you know it, your bare-knuckled pastime has turned into your livelihood; your getaway vehicle has become your sedan; your secret lair, your office.

In a fictional city of millions, there may be only a handful of caped crusaders. In real-life gothams, superheroes abound. Secret lives emerge from projects you're passionate about and from undiscovered talents that don't necessarily fit into day-to-day life. They may start off as a way to pass the time after work or as a quick weekend activity. But it blossoms from there.

Some avenues will fizzle out before you even hit the training montage. Others show promise, but something down the line causes you to hang up your cape: You might grow disillusioned; you might have to make the hero's choice and return to your normal life. Or maybe it fills a perfectly shaped metahuman hole in your life, happily coexisting with your daily activities.

And then there are the anomalies: the secret lives that slowly engulf the public ones. You don't really notice it creeping into your routine until it's already too late. Before you know it, your bare-knuckled pastime has turned into your livelihood; your getaway vehicle has become your sedan; your secret lair, your office. The mask isn't coming off any time soon.

A ship leaves a dying, apple-shaped planet

Every job I've held started in the shadows of a secret superhero life, and none more so than my work with *Macworld* magazine. Freelancers may understand the superhero comparison better than anyone, although it's more Mystery Men than Justice League. At any time, you might be called upon to don your mask, fling on your cape, and rush to the scene of the crime — or, in more practical terms, write 900 words on deadline.

You juggle your life, meals, evening outings, and day job as you wait for a signal to flash in the sky. And when it's been silent too long, you may even hunt danger on your own, hurling article proposals like fireballs into the ether with hopes of kindling interest. It's exhilarating.

But freelancing takes a toll on the lone avenger; very few can pour their lives into it for more than a couple of years without burning out. I hit my limit around the one-year mark. As luck would have it, *Macworld* was hiring. When I moved to San Francisco and started working for the magazine full-time, I was thrilled in many ways. But it turned my whirlwind of activity into a soft breeze. I no longer needed to fight for anything (except, perhaps, a seat on MUNI). And while I loved — and still love — my job, sometimes a little bit of chaos keeps passion in your life.

So one day, I walked into a warehouse in Oakland and became a superhero.

Portrait of a superhero on skates

Picture, if you will, a costume far less sleek than what you'd expect from your average Marvel or DC star. We may share the tights, but the similarities end there. I can't fly with a cape or engage super-speed; I use a pair of quad skates. My bones aren't Adamantium-laced; I use crash shorts, knee and elbow pads, wrist guards, a mouthpiece, and a helmet.

In short: I play roller derby.[1]

If you know me, it may seem like an odd fit. ("Ren? *Exercising?*") But I suspect that's why I like it. The sport — and it is a sport, contrary to what you might have seen back in the '80s[2] — is intentionally designed to let its participants compartmentalize. By day, we are neuroscientists, filmmakers, and woodworkers. We balance our high-stress jobs with sobriquets and larger-than-life personalities.[3] There are skaters who compete under their own names, but, even so, they transform on the track, leaving their off-skates selves on the sidelines. To get out on that oval, you have to be fearless.

That kind of mentality is almost antithetical to my daily routine. I don't like confrontation; I have doubts, worries, and concerns. When circumstances change abruptly, I stress out. But somehow, when I step on that track, it all falls away. The spinning of bearings and the screech of wheels against concrete drown out my anxiety.

I often play as jammer,[4] the only position that can score points. I am the target of at least four opposing players at any given time — and I love it. I revel in the quickness of the game, which forces me to dart through millisecond holes and pick apart movements. I can charge a wall of opposing players with no hesitation, leaping past muscled women and dancing on my skates' toe stops around those trying to knock me down.[5]

Who is Peter Parker without Spider-Man? Jean Grey without Phoenix? Bruce Wayne without Batman?

I like to think that part of the courage comes from anonymity: the ability to pull skates out of a gear bag and become someone else. But it's also that the derby community has built such an incredibly safe space for its players. Leagues are skater owned and operated, and nobody gets paid to put wheels on a track. We're all teaching each other, and we do it out of passion for the game. No one laughs at your first face-plant on the track; instead, we cringe in support, remembering our own rookie years. And it's a place where female athletes are celebrated, not treated as second class.[6]

It's empowering off the track, too. The athleticism alone required to participate in the sport forces me to cross-train with barbells and running shoes, and the mentality slips its way into my other projects. When you have nerves of steel on the track, it's hard for that confidence not to find its way into your interactions elsewhere.

The adventure continues

I've had adventures at all angles. I've tried out activities that left me uninterested within days. I have on-again, off-again flings with others. My day job was once my secret life; now my roller derby exploits keep it interesting. It's everything in balance that keeps my life in motion.

After all, who is Peter Parker without Spider-Man? Jean Grey without Phoenix? Bruce Wayne without Batman? Our projects and our passions — our superhero lives — let us keep our feet on the ground at other times. They push us to ask more questions, learn new things, and discover more about ourselves.

It's sometimes scary to have a hidden identity. The inner mystery pokes and pushes at areas of ourselves we don't want touched. But if you're willing to take the first step down that dark alley, you may just uncover your inner superhero.

1 Specifically, I play modern flat-track roller derby in the Boston Derby Dames, a league governed by the Women's Flat Track Derby Association (WFTDA). WFTDA has over 150 member leagues, and hosts yearly international tournaments for the top teams in the country. If you're interested in learning about the game, I suggest reading the WFTDA pages describing flat track and its gameplay. If you're curious to see a game, check WFTDA's member leagues to see if there's a venue near you. — RYV QST JVN FTT KVG

2 If you had the pleasure of watching *RollerJam* or *RollerGames*, I apologize. Please forget everything you learned from those shows, as modern roller derby is very little like that.

3 Derby names are intentionally pun-based and often replete with double and triple entendres. My favorite ones are those that manage to play off at least two of the following: the game, violence, and something that that person loves. (I have a soft spot in my heart for a blocker name I saw at my first

bout: Bloodbath and Beyond.) I skate under the name Artoo Detoonate. — SXH

4 Basic roller derby lesson #1: There are five players on each team — four blockers, one jammer — with 10 total players on the track. The jammer scores points by passing the hips of the opposing blockers; her blockers are there to aid her in scoring and to prevent the other team's jammer from scoring.

5 Basic roller derby lesson #2: Hitting zones. — DPY Blockers can only legally use their shoulders, hips, or booty to hit another player. Hits must be made above the knees and below the shoulders, and strictly on the front and sides — back blocks are illegal.

6 Unlike almost every other modern sport in existence, the roller derby revival began with leagues exclusive to women, and has continued that way throughout the years. There is a men's organization now — the Men's Roller Derby Association — but WFTDA is treated as the gold standard.

REDSHIRTS
IN THE COFFEE SHOP

This cosplay is pretty serious.

By GABE BULLARD

They're lined up five, six, seven deep on the streets of downtown Atlanta. Parents with small children on their shoulders, older folks in lawn chairs, pretty girls with their skinny boyfriends with cool haircuts. Tapping on their phones, posting photos.

Then there are sirens. The police clear the streets. They make room for the army. Storm Troopers, pirates, Doctors Who, and masses of other science fiction/fantasy/comic book characters march through the heart of the city in an unembarrassed display of the kind of nerdery that, years ago in most places and to this day in some, would have led to ostracism at best and being beaten up at worst.

It's the Dragon Con parade, the annual public showing of what happens inside five downtown hotels every Labor Day weekend in Atlanta. And the normies love it.

ZBM

Photos by Gabe Bullard

Carrie-ing on

Appeared in
Issue 26,
Sept. 26, 2013

Leah D'Andrea was in the parade. She's been coming to Dragon Con for over a decade. She pronounces her first name with a long a, like Leia. Like *Princess Leia*. She also looks like Carrie Fisher. A lot like Carrie Fisher. And she hasn't always liked *Star Wars*.

"I grew up hating it," she says. "Because of my name and because I was a brunette."

Then she saw the trench run from *A New Hope* on TV at a friend's house.[1] "I asked my friend's dad, 'What was that?' He said, '*Star Wars*.' I said, 'Seriously?! That's really cool.'" Two years later, D'Andrea, who already had an interest in theater and costumes, went to school dressed as Leia on Halloween.

"My teacher had a huge crush on Carrie Fisher because of *Star Wars*. When he saw me, he tried to sit down and missed his chair," she says. "I was kicked out of my history class that day."

A few years later, her now-husband, Chris Lee, proposed to her at a different convention with a replica of Leia's necklace from the movie. (It was even made by the same craftsman.) She was dressed as Leia; he was dressed as Luke Skywalker.[2]

At their home in Nashville, Lee is building components of a full-scale replica of the Millennium Falcon; D'Andrea makes costumes.[3] She's on her sixth version of the classic white "Leia dress." She has a Deanna Troi outfit. (In the appropriate wig, D'Andrea also looks a bit like Marina Sirtis, who played Troi on *Star Trek: The Next Generation*.) She has steampunk gear. She has comic book outfits. She can be a lot of people.

Make it sew

Wearing a costume is the ultimate expression of fandom, personally and publicly. Personally, you project yourself into a character in a way you can't through reading or watching. Publicly, it's a declaration that you relate to this fictional individual enough to embody him or her (or it).

"I think that's how most costumers get started," says D'Andrea. "They have a character they really, really admire." For D'Andrea, it was Princess Leia. For many of the attendees at Dragon Con, it appears to be Deadpool, from various Marvel Comics, or Finn from *Adventure Time*.[4]

RKS

MZG

Type http://magcode.me/ plus a blue code in the margin to visit the related Web page.

Some in the community differentiate between costuming and cosplay, a term derived from "costume play." Cosplay, they say, involves pretending to be a character, whereas costuming is dressing as that character but taking on no other traits.[5] But all of it falls on the same spectrum, as does the quality of the costumes. There are costumers and cosplayers who buy their gear from Halloween supply shops or the higher-quality fantasy outfitters, and there are those who, like D'Andrea, make their own.

A month before Dragon Con, I met D'Andrea in Nashville at the home of fellow costumers Steven and Gena Henderson. They and several others were preparing to craft and fine-tune the outfits and props they planned to take to the con. And it's not just about appearances. This stuff has to work.

"Leia's boots in *Return of the Jedi* looked like shoes with fabric stapled on them," says Steven. ("They were," D'andrea adds.) "We realized when we got into this, we're going to be walking through a crowd. We're going to have children tugging at it. It has to be perfect."

In movies, props and costumes are designed to look good on camera. The folks at Lucasfilm didn't have to worry about making something Leia could move around in for hours while holding on to her convention badge. "We have to be able to move in it," adds Gena. "And to pee in it," says D'Andrea.

D'Andrea, dressed as Angella, kneels before her comrades from Masters of the Universe.

So they make it better. It's a tribute and a challenge. And it's a thrill to gather with other costumers to compare techniques and details, of which there are many. D'Andrea's Leia Hoth suit is also an actual snowsuit. It's as warm as a freshly killed tauntaun. She has spent hours embroidering details into costumes that were never seen in the movies. And there's no disappointment in discovering the faults in movie props and costumes. Steven says it enhances the original: "I know things they don't know."

Who wants to imagine a future in which someone spends two minutes tightening bolts before taking flight?

D'Andrea is an actress, but no one in this group is costuming for profit. (Steven runs a software company; Gena works in medicine.) They're driven by fandom. They spend hours spinning fiction into fact with their costumes.[6] And it extends to characters that don't exist in popular fiction. D'Andrea won the 2012 Dragon Con masquerade, a costume contest, with a pair of steampunk wings designed by Lee that open and close with the aid of an app. Previously, any costume's wings were manually controlled. And who wants to imagine a future in which someone spends two minutes tightening bolts before taking flight?

Masters of the Universe

On my commuter-rail ride downtown on the Saturday of Dragon Con, I saw Jasmine from Aladdin taking a selfie. I saw a trio dressed as the heroes from *Final Fantasy VI* buying fare cards. I saw Hunter S. Thompson holding a piccolo (he was in a marching band in the parade). There they were, riding uneventfully alongside commuters headed to jobs, school, or sporting events.[7] And I felt out of place. I was dressed as me.

Outside the convention, the costume and the attendee badge are signals. They say "we're alike" the same way inside jokes on T-shirts have long communicated nerd status without shouting. It's a club.[8] "You don't have to get to know somebody, because you already know something about them," says D'Andrea.

This makes the con a ridiculously positive place. Spartans drink with Starfleet commanders. Marvel heroes and DC villains chat politely in lines for panel discussions. Everyone is excited, and no amount of geeking out is deemed excessive.

"People say, 'I finally get to wear my nerdy T-shirts, I'm going to a con.' I'm like, 'I get to wear my costumes and people know what they are,'" says Katrina Lynn, who was dressed as Carl Sagan (and not "sexy Carl Sagan") on the Sunday of Dragon Con.[9]

The costumes can be bulky or fragile, and the hotel's air conditioning isn't powerful enough to keep a crowd this size cool.

When I arrive at the con, I find D'Andrea walking through the Marriott lobby with over a dozen friends, all dressed in painstakingly detailed *Masters of the Universe* costumes. She dressed as Angella, with seven-foot-wide wings (non-motorized); Steven Henderson was He Man, complete with fur briefs.

They moved slowly. Every few feet, a conventioneer asked for a photo and the group obliged, drawing more photo seekers, larger crowds, and longer delays. With a group this big, stopping and posing isn't easy. The costumes can be bulky or fragile, and the hotel's air conditioning isn't powerful enough to keep a crowd this size cool. Some fans are costumers, looking to see how Sorceress made her cape.

"There's two schools of thought. There's pitch to the crowd and make them happy, and then there's hard-core costumers who try to impress each other," Chris Lee says as crowds rush past us to grab photos.

The con is spread out over five hotels. Every lobby, elevator, meeting room, and skywalk is packed with superheroes. So are the streets. Even in the frustrating southern summer sun, costumers pose on the sidewalks and order food at hip downtown restaurants. This is their world, but the normies inhabit it now too.

CONscription

"I went [to Dragon Con] 26 years ago. It was a bunch of guys playing Dungeons & Dragons and reading comics," says Miller Heath, who brought his two daugh-

ters to Dragon Con; all dressed in homemade costumes. "It's become much more accepted."

Many fans point to the 1939 World Science Fiction Convention as the first real convention for nerd culture. *Time* reported that 200 people came to the New York conference "for three days of speeches, pseudo-scientific movies, and discussion of stories with their authors." Some were in costume. About 130,000 people went to the San Diego Comic-Con in 2012 for similar purposes. Officials estimate that up to 60,000 came to Dragon Con this year. Many were in costume. (In contrast, at the PAX Prime event in Seattle in August 2013, only a handful of the 70,000-plus attendees came in costume. They were mostly there to play games.)

No one points to any single cause for the rising interest, but it's there. If nerdery, even in private, were fringe behavior, then it would be difficult to explain why out of the 10 highest-grossing movies of all time (not adjusted for inflation), all but two are centered on superheroes, science fiction, or fantasy.[10]

It's likely that many of the contributors to the billion-dollar gross of a superhero movie are only casually interested. But if they want to know more about, let's say, Tony Stark, they can fall down a very deep, very interesting rabbit hole on Wikipedia. They can learn more about characters with decades-long histo-

ries. They can discover that many more people are also interested in these characters. They can form relationships with those characters. They can take this interest into meatspace at a convention. And, as their interest develops, they can decide to embody a beloved character; they can costume at a con.

"There's an atmosphere of no judgment," says Neil Gibson, a comic book author promoting his work at the convention. "Some people like the characters and want to dress up as them. Some people see it as a day out. Some people take it very competitively and want to have the best costume there is. Whatever you're into is great."

I asked many conventioneers why they think the popularity has grown, and none of them knew. They were all just happy it was happening.

"All these things I didn't like before — parties, socializing, clubs — turns out I just didn't like the people at them," says Steven Henderson.

Fantastic fore-bears

There are lots of children, some in strollers and some in spandex, on the convention floor.[11] Parents are bringing their kids into geek culture. There are many, many people in costume, and many, many more not in costume, taking it all in. It can be overwhelming to see how popular geek culture has become.

Not everyone who wears costumes and reads comics books is teased growing up, but for many, it's hard to fit in as a geek, and it's not easy to see your thing become everyone's thing. But now that the levitation boot is on the other foot, the nerds aren't exactly taking revenge.

"At some point I grew out of [rejecting new geeks]," says Lynn. "If you have that attitude, it's like you're saying to everybody that they can't belong to this little club. That this club is for people who have gone through bad things. But it's not. What it is, is a club for people who like stuff, for people who are happy and passionate. It should be a positive club." (Comedian Patton Oswalt had a slightly different take on the matter in a *Wired* essay in 2010, arguing that geeks should fight against mainstream appropriation of the symbols of their obsessions — "Boba Fett's helmet emblazoned on sleeveless T-shirts worn by gym douches" — but not against appreciation of those things.)

If nerdery were fringe behavior, then why are 8 of the 10 all-time highest-grossing movies centered on superheroes, science fiction, or fantasy.

D'Andrea says there's been a slight shift in tone at conventions over the years, but it's stamped out rather quickly. "It's not so much jocks versus nerds. It's the people who come just to party versus the people who come to panels," she says. "You get your standard shit-talkers. It's like any crowd of people; you're going to get your jackasses. But we're all here for the same thing."

And who can say costuming is so unusual anyway? Every day, people put on sports jerseys without ever getting onto a field. "It's acceptable to paint your face and stand at a football game," says Gena Henderson. "So why not paint your face and stand around at a hotel?" asks D'Andrea. "Everyone has that category of nerd," says Steven Henderson. "And yours might just be universally accepted."

"And ours is becoming universally accepted," says D'Andrea.

CONplications

There are risks to making the unreal real, and there are risks to outsiders flooding in. They're called creepers. The first time D'Andrea dressed as Leia, it distracted her history teacher. She was in the white dress from *A New Hope*. But while the bun hairdo has certainly appeared in many fantasies, it kneels before the Zod of Star Wars sexiness: the gold bikini.

D'Andrea has worn the Leia slave outfit at conventions. She knows what it can represent to some male fans. "Whenever you put something on like that, you're the center of attention," she says, admitting that she's been inappropriately approached and touched while in costume. "But the appropriateness with how people react is a lot better at a convention than it is in the real world. I've been leched on in public more than I ever have at a con in costume."

"The people who don't get it are newer to fandom, newer to conventions," says longtime costumer Katrina Lynn. "They don't understand the women that are in these costumes — mostly it's women — are there for themselves. They're not getting paid to be there and be touched on. That's been their experience with scantily clad women. They work at Hooters. They're strippers. I think people don't realize there's a disconnect."

Many female characters were conceived of and drawn by men. They serve as objects of fantasy for men. They wear costumes that are impossibly skimpy.

Many female characters were conceived of and drawn by men. They serve as objects of fantasy for men. They wear costumes that are impossibly skimpy. They stand in ridiculous poses that show off rear ends and breasts at the same time. They are characters that are born objectified. But that doesn't mean women can't relate to other characteristics.

"There's an effort to obtain the impossible in cosplay," says Hannah Burnett, who runs the Cosplay Safety Project. "I don't see why unrealistic proportions and gravity-defying things should keep anyone away from a character design. If that's the character you want to embody, if that's how you want to express yourself, more power to you. Just understand you might want a bodyguard with you sometimes."

Women who wear the more revealing costumes turn the original objectivity on its ear. But at every convention, there are creepers turning it right back by copping feels and taking photos exclusively of bikini-clad bottoms.

"There are people who, for whatever reason, can't conceptualize what is so wrong about it," says Burnett. She was on a Dragon Con panel on ethics in cosplay, and she recommended directly addressing creepers if they try anything on a convention floor. She also referenced a group called Cosplay Is Not Consent, which fights objectification of female costumers.

D'Andrea, Lynn, and Burnett agree that creeping is an issue, but that it happens to them outside of conventions when they're wearing street clothes, too. That it happens in regular life doesn't make it something anyone wants to live with. Burnett is hopeful. She says there's progress in the convention world, because in the mutual-appreciation atmosphere of the con, the conversation can happen.

Doctor, nothing will stop it!

There's a hat that's ever-present at Dragon Con. It's a knitted stocking cap with earflaps and a puff at the top. It's colored in yellow and orange stripes. It's a coded message to fans of the TV show *Firefly*. A character named Jayne Cobb briefly wears a similar hat in one popular scene.

There's a reward to understanding the meaning behind someone's hat. There's a small thrill that happens a thousand times a second at Dragon Con whenever someone recognizes a reference or figures out that the guy with a blaster wearing a red plastic cylinder is Han Solo Cup. And as newbies and former normies fill the convention space, the veterans work harder to show their experience.

As her husband, dressed as He Man, guides a dozen Masters of the Universe through the Marriott lobby, Gena Henderson, in a Supergirl costume, says it's hard to pull off big-group excursions like this, because it's difficult to find something new. And some costumes have become so easy to put together that they're everywhere (I lost count of the number of Finn hats I saw).

"We have to keep raising the bar," says D'Andrea. Her costume is impressive; it's one of many fantastic outfits put together for no reason other than to show off to others. There's no money for this, though D'Andrea did win cash and an iPad for her wings at last year's masquerade costume contest. There's no greater fame that comes from being the most realistic Hulk or the cutest Pikachu. But for the costumed folks surrounding me in the Marriott, it's what they like.

As I watched Henderson and D'Andrea pose in their costumes, facing camera flashes more reminiscent of an LA paparazzi scrum than a He Man cartoon, I felt an infectious, overwhelmingly positive feeling wash over me. I'd always liked Nightcrawler. Maybe I could find some blue face paint and a plush tail at the gift shop. Then I was pulled back into reality by a tired Eternian.

"Even the backs of my legs are sweaty."

It's not always easy being a hero.

1 This is the climactic flight scene near the end of the movie when, spoiler alert, Luke Skywalker blows up the Death Star.

2 Someone in the crowd pointed out that the two were playing characters who are, spoiler alert, siblings.

3 Nathan Meuiner wrote about Lee's project in "Full Scale," in Issue 18 (June 6, 2013) of The Magazine.

4 And this doesn't mean you have to look like the character you play. There are many costumers who play something other than their actual gender, body type, skin color, and so on. It's called crossplaying.

5 And there were people I talked to at Dragon Con who refused to break character. One man, dressed as Xerxes from the movie 300, frequently said, "Why doesn't anyone like me?"

6 This extends to their bodies, too. The Hendersons and D'Andrea diet and exercise to maintain the proper proportions for costumes. "The best thing you can do to keep yourself in shape is wear spandex on a regular basis," says Steven.

7 There is a football game of significance in Atlanta on Labor Day weekend, too.

8 Another spoiler alert: I'm going to use the words "nerd" and "geek" in the remainder of this article. I don't do it pejoratively. I use them interchangeably to mean enthusiasts, experts, and general lovers of this stuff. The community has embraced the terms. They're compliments, not insults.

9 This might be a redundant phrase to many.

10 If you count James Bond as a superhero, then nine of the top 10 are about superheroes, science fiction, or fantasy. They would all fall into one of these categories if you count Titanic as fantasy, but that's a bit of a stretch.

11 As the evening wears on, children are advised to leave the main convention spaces. The people I talked to agree that Dragon Con is the hardest-partying con, and the alcohol and sexy costumes are hard to avoid after dark.

PZJ

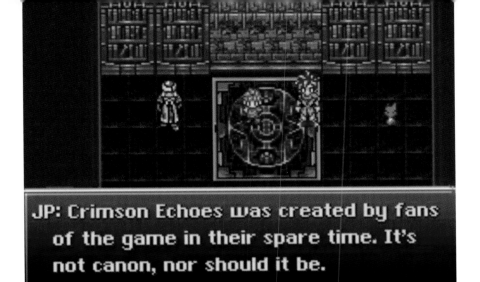

JP: Crimson Echoes was created by fans of the game in their spare time. It's not canon, nor should it be.

The Everending Story

The greatest video game sequel never authorized remains incomplete.

By KEVIN PURDY

It was to be less than a month until four young men, spread across the world but united in purpose, would do something almost nobody gets to do: fix a part of their life that a major media conglomerate had callously abandoned.

If their obsession had been a favorite film, one with a few plot holes and loose narrative threads, it would have been daunting and unrewarding to obtain a film crew, funding, and the time off to shoot their own incongruous pick-up scenes. The same goes for albums, which require master copies and a talented ear, or books and board games, which demand immense time and skill to improve on or extend in a meaningful way.

But this team's particular obsession was a Super Nintendo game, and they had learned what made it tick through five years of crowd-sourced scrutiny and endless

Appeared in Issue 23, Aug. 15, 2013

A screen capture from Crimson Echoes

trial and error. From the core of the acclaimed game *Chrono Trigger*, they had built an epic, unofficial sequel: *Chrono Trigger*: *Crimson Echoes*. It had 23 chapters and 13 possible endings, and added up to 35 hours of gameplay. They would release it for free, and give *Chrono Trigger* lovers something rare: a chance to go on new adventures with characters they deeply cared for, and to finish the story they knew so well.

There was ZeaLitY, a Texan writer with a rabid hunger for *Chrono* knowledge and continuity; Chrono'99, a French modder with a knack for tricky choreographed scenes who had one ROM hack hit under his belt; Agent 12, a West Coast professional developer who programmed and bug-fixed at a seemingly inhuman pace; and a handful of others, including FaustWolf, an eloquent and fastidious graphics worker and beta tester. They were mostly college or graduate school age, and they had kept their work under wraps, with a few teases here and there.

The storyline follows a trio of spirited youths who accidentally travel through time, learn of a great disaster in the future, and set out to stop it.

But on May 9, 2009, with three weeks to go until launch, Agent 12 spoke with a lawyer from *Chrono Trigger*'s maker, Square Enix, who explained the details of the cease-and-desist letter the firm had sent with clipped yes-or-no certainty: delete everything or be bankrupted.

They complied. Their reward for destroying their dream was to become the targets of account hacking, social engineering attempts, and seemingly endless online harassment by former fans. They were branded incompetent cowards, forgers, liars, and, perhaps worst of all, betrayers of the *Chrono* legacy.

How had fandom come to such a punishing result?

Forward to the past

The company then known as Squaresoft (and sometimes just "Square") released *Chrono Trigger* in 1995, at the height of its creative powers and during the "golden age" of Japanese roleplaying games. Akira Toriyama, the artist behind the best-selling manga series *Dragon Ball*, crafted the characters and visual style.

The score, by Yasunori Mitsuda and *Final Fantasy* stalwart Nobuo Uematsu, became an instant gaming classic, spawning hundreds of orchestral and fan remix versions. Most significantly, the main writer, Masato Kato, brought a novelist's touch to an intricate, epic time-travel plot. Many fans have yet to see a story anything like what they saw in *Chrono Trigger*.

Lifehacker writer Adam Dachis, who has played through *Chrono Trigger* at least 20 times and witnessed every ending, says the game "follows classic film story structure better than any other (roleplaying game) I've played." *Chrono Trigger* mattered so much to Phill Spiess that his girlfriend played through it to get to know him — and he proposed to her by hacking a part of the game. *Crimson Echoes* leader ZeaLitY credits his obsession to the game's "tenor and spirit." (ZeaLitY spoke on condition that his offline name not be used.)

"It's crammed with a vigor that most games, as most movies, have a hard time maintaining through the entire story," ZeaLitY writes via email.

The storyline follows a trio of spirited youths who accidentally travel through time, learn of a great disaster in the future, and set out to stop it, meeting companions and enemies along the way. But such a quick summary leaves out an inventor father who accidentally cripples his wife, imbuing their genius daughter with a desire to fix both devices and people. It ignores the child prince who becomes a conflicted, revenge-driven villain. And it says nothing about a moment, roughly halfway through, when the tone, gameplay, and goals all change.

Chrono Trigger sold two million Super Nintendo cartridges in Japan, a solid performance for the time, and roughly 280,000 in the United States, where it could cost up to $80. A 2000 PlayStation follow-up, *Chrono Cross*, was set in the same world and written with Kato's help, but was a loosely connected non-sequel. A 2001 trademark that Squaresoft registered for "*Chrono Break*" expired after a decade's time. Meanwhile, *Trigger* continues to be re-released for new platforms and mobile app stores, with very minor changes or upgrades.

Trigger's key craftsman seems haunted, or maybe tortured, by the idea of returning to his creation. He wrote a dark and quirky text-based adventure, *Radical Dreamers*, for an obscure satellite-based Super Nintendo add-on, but later tried to halt and disown it.[1] Interviewed for a guidebook to *Cross*, Kato said there were *Trigger* elements to build on, but "the sense of dancing you get from exploring [those] worlds is a little more difficult to capture than I initially thought.... If we try to do a sequel, I want to perfect that completely."

And that, roughly, is where *Crimson Echoes* came in.

Trial run

RCC

In 2003, ZeaLitY created the wiki-style Chrono Compendium site, a truly comprehensive take on all things in the *Chrono* continuum. It quickly became a hub for discussion and complaining about the lack of new projects. Excitement built up for two attempted 3D remakes, *Chrono Resurrection* and *Remake Project*, until they were both shut down by cease-and-desist letters from Square Enix, a merger of Squaresoft with Enix, best known for *Dragon Quest*.

YLR, ZLN

But then, in late 2004, a hacker named Geiger released a stable version of Temporal Flux, a tool that made it far more of a step-by-step process to hack the ROM in *Chrono Trigger* to isolate its game engine than had previous complicated stabs in the dark.[2] (An engine sits at the heart of any game, and it renders elements onscreen, controls interactions, and manages the physics, among other tasks.)

WPF
ZKB

It still wasn't easy, and it could feel like fixing a car engine through a glove compartment, but Geiger put most of the original developers' powers into the hands of fans. Ideas, goofs, and a coliseum-style battle game showed up on the Compendium, but nothing substantial until 2007. That's when ZeaLitY posted the plot and scenarios he had spent years refining, and made some earnest pleas for help. He assembled a team, created a private forum, and everybody's free time took a big hit.

ZeaLitY wrote thousands of lines of dialogue, both for big plot moments and for one-time interactions. Agent 12 programmed and tore through many, many bugs, along with managing the project. Chrono'99 staged scenarios and worked out the if-then mechanics. FaustWolf helped with turning fan-generated art into pixels and polishing the game's rough patches. They released a one-off,

NTZ

two-chapter game, *Prophet's Guile*, mostly to give themselves a break and generate excitement, and it saw roughly 25,000 downloads. By early 2009, ZeaLitY says, the team was cranking. "We were looking at a workable [*Crimson*] product."

What lies beyond?

The plot of *Crimson Echoes* picks up five years after *Chrono Trigger*'s ending. There is no elevator-pitch version of this plot. Understanding the quests and character motivations requires robust familiarity with the original. There are striking sequences, touching bits of dialogue, winking nods, and clever uses of time-travel logic, but also some odd creations and plot directions. It tackles, ZeaLitY says, "mysteries and unexplained plot points, and [missing] character development" from the original. Like most *Chrono* fans I spoke with, I found it intriguing, and satisfying for its connection of disparate *Trigger* and *Cross* elements, but the show/tell ratio is heavily imbalanced toward the latter.

Crimson Echoes feels unfinished, in part, because it is. I played though about five hours of a "98 percent finished" beta version, and viewed the rest of the nar-

---

Excitement built up for two attempted 3D remakes, Chrono Resurrection *and* Remake Project, *until they were both shut down by cease-and-desist letters from Square Enix.*

rative on a "CEMemorial" YouTube playlist. The letter sent by Square Enix on May 8, 2009, threatened damages of "up to $150,000 per work." It was a not-for-profit project, and the finished game would have required a copy of an original *Trigger* ROM (theoretically a backup copy) to play, but nobody could afford the legal fight.

Some aspects of ROM hacking, such as the legality of backup copies and modifying games for accessibility and interoperability, remain undefined by the courts. On the hackers' side, there was the 1992 US District Court ruling in *Galoob v. Nintendo*, which found that Game Genie's creation of "new variations of play" was a fair-use case. But nearly every attorney I asked about the case of *Crimson Echoes* noted two issues: unauthorized derivative works, and the license agreements that accompany game purchases.

"If the 'mod' constitutes a modification of the game...and it includes substantial portions of the original game, then it may constitute a derivative work or a reproduction which may constitute copyright infringement," says Kurt E. Anderson, an attorney at the New Jersey firm Giordano Halleran and Ciesla who specializes in software and copyright issues. "The terms of the license may [also] prohibit hacking and modifying the backup copy, and would likely prohibit further distribution of copies."

Square Enix's attorney didn't explain that, or much of anything, when he spoke to Agent 12 on a Friday night in early May 2009. The lawyer, according to *Crimson* team members, said that the letter had "come down from Japan," but

MDY

ZYT

WVD

initially offered to push Square Enix into making an official statement — if the team could stay mostly silent. The team took the mod forum down with a terse announcement. But after days of back and forth, the company changed its tune. There would be no statement and no game. The *Crimson* team felt it couldn't name names at Square Enix, for fear that those named would "get the entire 4Chan treatment" (as ZeaLitY put it), destroying their last chance at dialogue with the company.

"The reason why I was ethically OK with releasing it was that I considered it in very poor taste to kill such a large project that was so close to completion." — LESTER

The end of time

Instead, the team itself received the threats and hacking attempts, and they were accused of faking the Square letter to get out of a full release. Very few fans approached with constructive help; many more suggested mistakes in the *Crimson Echoes* team's legal and coding strategies. Ryan Lester renewed the fans' hopes by leaking an earlier copy of *Crimson* onto Reddit's gaming section. Spurred by a new sense of us-versus-Big-Corporate-them urgency, a smaller team of programmers tweaked the music, added weapons and endings, and released the remixed work in 2011 as *Flames of Eternity*.

HVM
LMP

Lester, now a developer at SpaceX and the creator of music streaming service Peer.fm, tells me via email that no pseudonym is necessary; he gladly owns up to leaking *Crimson Echoes*, despite understanding the risks and somewhat sympathizing with Square Enix's legal obligations.

"The reason why I was ethically OK with releasing it was that I considered it in very poor taste to kill such a large project that was so close to completion," Lester explains. "The finished project is nothing short of brilliant, 100 percent worthy of being accepted as canon."

For its makers, *Crimson Echoes* has a multi-headed legacy. Most members of the team have distanced themselves from the game (and would not speak for this article). It doesn't help that the makers of *Flames of Eternity* openly mocked the originators and introduced incongruities that irked the *Crimson* team. Yet there are always modifications to be made. There is chatter about an outside team still working on finishing *Crimson Echoes* in the spirit of its original plans. Another project that learned a lot from *Crimson Echoes* — especially its potential legal liability — is trying to remake *Chrono Trigger* using modern graphics, but the team has no Web site and is strictly pseudonymous. And although Square Enix killed the project, *Crimson Echoes* at least forced the firm to acknowledge the hunger of *Chrono* fans for more gameplay, more answers.

NKZ

The five-year effort might also serve as a waypoint marker in the history of game development, and of Japanese roleplaying games in particular. A place where, to paraphrase Hunter S. Thompson, you could see where the creative wave finally broke and rolled back.

"In the past you had the big names, like Hironobu Sakaguchi and Masato Kato and high-profile artists, who could push through a project and be supported," ZeaLitY says. "Nowadays you have this faceless kind of franchise development model: hire all the gaming team, and as soon as the product ships, fire them all, or wait for the next project from the board of directors."

If nothing else, ZeaLitY says, *Chrono Trigger* and *Chrono Cross* have been united in story, and crucial bits of backstory explained. Most people can't see it and don't know about it, but the fixes are in. And enough code has been spread around that somebody might still be revisiting and revising this quirky piece of gaming history.

---

1 Incidentally, that obscurity, and the rarity of Satellaview games in general, makes *Radical Dreamers* one of the most valuable games in Tokyo's Akihabara used-game district – roughly the 13th most expensive, according to Wired. RFX

2 Although ROM (read-only memory) chips are permanently burned with a program's software, the software can be loaded and patched, and it can then be used on an emulator or even burned (via EEPROM or other means) into a new cartridge.

HOEDOWN

SMALL-SCALE FARMERS HAVE TURNED TO HIGH TECH TO INVENT THE TOOLS THEY NEED.

By **CARA PARKS** | When Eliot Coleman started out as a small-scale farmer in 1966, he had little more than a small rototiller and some hoes. At a loss for tools designed for his needs, Coleman began modifying them himself, beginning with one of his hoes. "I took it into the shop, bent the shaft a little bit, cut parts off or welded parts on, and the next thing I knew I had a much better hoe."

Above: A collinear hoe. **Courtesy of Johnny's Select Seeds**
At left: A farm grows in Brooklyn — and Queens. **Photos by Cara Parks**

The collinear hoe remains popular, a cult favorite in the small-farming and large-gardening communities. It's designed to let the user stand erect while using the implement more like a broom, and its compact head allows for accuracy in small spaces. Traditional, heavy hoes require the user to bend over uncomfortably and are designed for less precise work.

Eliot Coleman went on to write *The New Organic Grower* and other books that have become canonical texts for small growers — roughly, those with under five acres. He says the last time anyone made tools for that scale of operation was the 19th century, when such farms abounded.

"There are two other 19th-century industries that are still around today, and it's hand-thrown pottery and hand-woven rugs. The hand-throw potters don't compete with Tupperware. The hand-woven rug people don't compete with Burlington Mills. But the small vegetable farmer is competing with the big vegetable farmer," Coleman says.

Eager farmers have turned into innovators as they try to use technological know-how to obviate some of the necessary hard work while improving efficiency.

For nearly half a century, Coleman has been inventing tools and discovering efficient products made around the world. Recently, he has agitated for more farmers to work collectively to, as it were, build a better hoe. "I've always noticed that when you get a bunch of small farmers together and they start kicking an idea around, you can make unbelievable progress," Coleman says. "That's why it was a good idea to get a lot of the tool geeks together. The farm-tool geeks."

Growing new tools

Fewer than two percent of Americans are full-time farmers today, but an idealistic image of farming remains. Thomas Jefferson declared that "those who labour in the earth are the chosen people of God." While office drones may dream of a contemplative life of breaking sod in nearly unbroken silence, the reality of farming is that it has always been and remains hard work.

Eager farmers have turned into innovators as they try to use technological know-how to obviate some of the necessary hard work while improving efficiency, and thus make small farms potentially viable, either as a stand-alone business or as part of the way a farmer makes a living.

At Coleman's suggestion, the Stone Barns Center for Food and Agriculture has been holding meetings of tool geeks for the last two years. Called the Slow Tools Project, it connects engineers with farmers to come up with appropriately scaled tools. Stone Barns is heavily involved in nurturing and training young farmers, whom Jill Isenbarger, the Center's executive director, describes as "modern-day Thomas Jeffersons" who are combining science, technology, and philosophy with agriculture. She wants the program to underscore the role that innovation plays in small farming and fight the public perception of farming as a throwback profession. "It's not just, 'Come here and learn to raise a chicken on some grass,'" she says. "We are teaching them to weld; we are teaching them to tinker."

The Center's head grower, Jack Algiere, is working on an electric tractor with the Small Tools team. Its current incarnation is tucked into a workshop under the Center's bustling main buildings. A jumble of parts and ideas, the prototype is meant to be "cut up and Frankenstein-ed around a little bit," but its basic shape is coming into focus, drawing on existing industries for components: the transmission and motor from a zero-turn lawnmower; durable trailer hitches; and basic tractor wheels.

While the young farmers Algiere meets usually don't have the early exposure to machinery that he grew up with — changing the oil on a car and other basic mechanic work — he's not worried about their changing skill-set. "We understand plug-and-play, and that's what our revolution is," he says of the next generation of farmers. "That is what new technology is. It's smart motors, wireless remote things. Batteries, motors; not engines."

Small growers know what technology they need, but despair at finding tools both compact and cheap enough. The lithium batteries now used in electric cars could give a solar tractor enough horsepower to pull a farm implement, but they are currently prohibitively expensive. "It's at our fingertips," Algiere says of this next level of technology. However, manufacturers must be convinced that by diverting even minor resources toward developing small-scale tools, they would be rewarded with a large enough and supremely loyal set of customers.

Some businesses are already catering to this small but significant niche market. (About one percent of farmland in the United States is made up of farms

SKN

GTP

⧓

Appeared in
Issue 22,
Aug. 1, 2013

DKC

under 10 acres.) Johnny's Selected Seeds, which operates near Coleman's farm in Maine, is a leader in the small-scale tool field. Adam Lemieux, Johnny's tools and supplies manager, has watched interest in this field expand. "In the last 10 years there's been a lot of push toward scale-appropriate tools for small commercial growers," he says. To respond to this newfound interest, Johnny's aims to design new tools that can revolutionize the way some small farms operate, even if it means, as he says, "reinventing the wheel."

Recently, the company began selling a small-greens harvester, "a tough nut to crack," according to Lemieux. With early versions of the tool, small salad greens became wedged together as they were cut and didn't drop into a harvesting basket. Coleman and Lemieux tinkered with the idea off and on for years, until a teenage farmer from Tennessee spoke with Coleman and decided to take a crack at the problem.

Jonathan Dysinger's design uses two stainless-steel bandsaw blades that were designed to cut through frozen boneless meat. It turns out that this form of blade has scallops just deep enough to tackle the average salad-green stem. He also added a brush that pushes the greens through the blades and into the waiting basket. Dysinger's Quick Cut Greens Harvester is a huge time-saver for small farmers.

Lemieux feels that it's not a shortage of creativity but a shortage of market possibilities that inhibits most small-farm tech. Some farms are victims of path dependence, having adjusted their growing methods to work with outdated tools. Others are just uninformed about their options. "The collinear hoe is a good example of that," he says. "It's one of our customers' favorite products, and it's my favorite hoe for sure. It kind of does everything, and it does it very, very well. But you still don't see them. You go into True Value and you're not going to see one."

Dysinger's Quick Cut Greens Harvester

Cool heads prevail

The USDA has found, unsurprisingly, that profitability is intimately tied to farm size. Small farms wage a daily battle against economies of scale, and poorly scaled tools can be a major impediment. "Because we don't have tools that are appropriately sized we buy a more expensive, larger thing that doesn't [work] as well as something we can envision," explains Algiere.

WYW

Groups like Farm Hack are attempting to connect farmers and engineers, both online and on the ground, to create new tools and solutions, but the small-farming community is always looking for more know-how. "There's a lot of opportunity for young technical guys to get into that part of agriculture — making tools as a support mechanism," says Algiere.

MTK

Ron Khosla left the technology industry to farm with his wife in New Paltz, New York. He focused on solving inefficiencies in an effort to compete as much as possible with conventional growers. Khosla approached day-to-day farm problems with a "better living through technology" philosophy.

Johnny's aims to design new tools that can revolutionize the way some small farms operate, even if it means reinventing the wheel.

One early success was the CoolBot, a controller that allows farmers to create walk-in coolers using a 10,000-BTU air conditioner, the type that dots New York high rises during summer months. Using a series of sensors, the controller tricks the air conditioner into lowering the temperature well below where an AC unit normally shuts off, while also keeping the unit from icing over. While it sounds simple enough, this device can save a small farmer thousands of dollars. Khosla says he has sold over 12,000 of the controllers. (The CoolBot is $299 plus the price of an air conditioner, whereas traditional coolers run in the thousands.)

RSQ

He also worked on other energy-efficient techniques, such as using warm water piped under plants to warm seedlings in a greenhouse. Khosla estimates that this system reduced his fuel outlay by 90 percent, a savings of about $2,000 a month for the 1,500-square-foot greenhouse.

But Khosla, who has gone on to serve as an advisor to the United Nations Food and Agricultural Organization, realized that the greatest impact came from making his own labor more efficient by ruthlessly tracking metrics on nearly every aspect of plant cultivation. "We went from taking 25 seconds per plant to working and working and working until it was 1.3 seconds per transplant," he says. That type of efficiency helped make his farm profitable. "Farming is a count-your-seconds activity," he says.

On the other hand, there is a middle ground between impractical time expenditures and a single-minded focus on the bottom line. Josh Volk, who often begins his days with a 26-mile bicycle ride to Our Table Cooperative just outside of Portland, Oregon, designed and oversees its vegetable growing operation. Volk's background is in mechanical tool design, which he enjoyed but ultimately found unfulfilling, along with his office in a "concrete bunker."

Although he has helped set up electric tractor systems for other farms and currently uses a two-wheel tractor at Our Table, he spent years running a farm using only hand tools. (To meet the needs of small farms, he also designed a modified garden cart, a few of which are in heavy rotation at Our Table.) Volk believes that design should focus on expanding the abilities of the user. Focusing on the economic outcome? "Those are two separate goals," he says. "I think the better goal is to improve ergonomics and to let people do things they weren't able to do before."

One taste of the ethereal blueberries growing along his vegetable patch — Platonic ideals of the fruit, all mellow sweetness waiting to burst through a thin skin — suggests he might be on to something.

Sunbathing

Brooklyn Grange, nestled in the borough's recently revitalized Navy Yards, is an example of how these tools can coalesce into one high-performing operation. Immaculately dressed young men and women jump on and off the elevator that eventually leads to an Oz-like shift from drab industrial flooring into rows of Technicolor flowers, emerald salad greens, and multi-hued carrots. Housed on two rooftops — one in Brooklyn and one in Queens — the two-and-a-half-acre farm has sold more than 40,000 pounds of vegetables, according to its founders.

On one side of the roof, the temperature of a repurposed shipping container is regulated by a CoolBot. A shed standing in relief against the New York skyline houses a greens harvester and a collinear hoe, while a few yards away stands a

greenhouse, one of the first of its kind for a rooftop garden. (The greenhouse was specially designed by another engineer-turned-farmer, Greg Garbos of Four Season Tools, who formerly worked for Ford.)

Ben Flanner, one of the farm's co-founders and its head grower, has been running the consistently profitable farm for four years. The 32-year-old has a degree in industrial engineering, "which is processes, time, and motion," he says. In addition to the tools in use here, the Queens location boasts a solar-powered forced-air composting system. The group is also hoping to invest soon in some tilthers, which quickly and efficiently mix soil additives into the top few layers of soil and break up roots, like a shallow tiller ("a fantastic product that is grossly overpriced because it's not made offshore," says Lemieux).

Despite the incredible ingenuity of farmers today, many gaps remain to be filled, especially by those with technical and engineering skills. An influx of ergonomic, properly scaled, and energy-efficient tools designed specifically with the needs of small farms in mind would help growers across the country survive in a difficult market.

"I think that some of the biggest manufacturers are going to realize that there's a market for this," Lemieux says. And of course, farmers will continue to help one another. After all, Thomas Jefferson also said, "I think it the duty of farmers who are wealthier than others to give those less so the benefit of any improvements they can introduce, gratis."

Tiny Furniture

A smaller house expanded our view.

By THADDEUS HUNT

Appeared in
Issue 19,
June 20, 2013

The din of the birthday party and the screams of 15 five-year-olds were still ringing in our ears. Once inside the car, however, all we heard was the A/C blasting and the sound of US Highway 1 rolling by underneath. We love children, but this quiet was beautiful. Somewhere along the drive home, my wife, Melinda, broke the silence.

"You know?" She paused.

"Yeah?" I said, glancing over and then back at the road.

"I really don't want to have children."

It wasn't the words that surprised me; we were both approaching our late twenties. We'd had this discussion several times already. It was the delivery: heavy, calculated, and, above all, honest.

I didn't look at her because I knew she was staring, as I was, straight ahead, looking right down that highway.

"I really don't want children either," I said. Like her, I meant it.

Of all the times we'd talked about kids and the possibility of skipping parenthood, this time honestly felt like the last time.

It turned out that it was.

Illustration by Dominic Flask

Sudden shift

That brief conversation altered everything in our lives. Chief among the changes was our concept of space. Suddenly, without kids on the horizon, everything we owned seemed gratuitous. It wasn't long before we started to do something about it. Able to carpool to our shared employer, two cars became one. We took leaf-bags of clothing to Goodwill. I quickly became intimately familiar with Freecycle.org and Craigslist. Anything we hardly used, we gave away or sold.

GYL, LRY

It wasn't long before we turned our eyes on our house, which suddenly appeared quite empty. There was absolutely nothing wrong with the home — or the neighborhood — in which we'd spent the last decade. We bought the property with the full intention of having kids to run around in the backyard, jump through sprinklers, and play with their neighbors. Hell, we even chose the area because of the schools that were nearby.

But that need was now definitively gone. The house had provided us with a lot of good memories, but it was full of empty rooms where we spent little or no time, and its closets were jammed with junk we couldn't recall buying. When we factored in the time and utilities needed to take care of all that unused space, it was a no-brainer. We had to make a change. We had to move.

Big news, tiny plans

It was March 2012, and the housing market was just starting to heal when we called a real-estate agent. Everyone thought we were crazy, but we had made up our minds. Our house no longer felt like home, and we didn't see the point in staying there any longer. We cleaned and tidied and made the house sale-worthy, put a sign out front, and hoped for the best.

Four months went by before we had a buyer. One evening in mid-July, as I was bringing out the trash, a neighbor who had seen the red "Under Contract" slate perched on top of the real-estate agent's sign came over to congratulate me and ask what was next for us. I told him that we were moving to Durham to be closer to work.

"You guys getting a bigger place?" he asked. "I couldn't believe it when I read the square footage on this one." He nodded toward what would soon be someone else's home.

"Actually, we're planning on downsizing," I said, by now expecting what came next.

"Downsizing?! Really?" He raised his eyebrows.

At this point, I'd had this conversation at least a dozen times. People couldn't believe that we were actually considering a smaller home. When I confided to our closest friends that we were, in fact, looking for something half the size or smaller? Well, that typically tipped even the folks who knew us best over the edge. We got everything from "Oh my, I couldn't do that at all" to "Have you guys really thought this through?"

My favorite, typically whispered, comment was, "What if you just need time alone?" We just chuckled every time. It was as if everyone wanted us to slow down, to think it over. We, however, couldn't wait.

And we didn't.

"You guys getting a bigger place?" "Actually, we're planning on downsizing." "Downsizing?! Really?" He raised his eyebrows.

Next in line

Since we had only a month to find a new home, we began scouring ads in search of deals and move-in specials. We wanted to rent, so we aimed high and searched for studios and lofts in the downtown area. There wasn't much, but we didn't give up. Despite all the tools that had proliferated in the 11 years since we'd moved to the suburbs and last had to consult them, it was old-fashioned Craigslist that led us to a winner after a lot of looking — via PadMapper.com, which pulls data from Craigslist.

It was 500 square feet, affordable, a six-minute walk from my office, and an even shorter distance to everything else we could possibly want. It seemed wonderful! We called, landed third on the wait list, and hoped. Two days later, the owner called us back to ask if we were still interested. He said the size of the place caused the folks in front of us to withdraw from the running.

We grabbed a tape measure and hopped back in the car. Our daily commute from Apex to Durham was 45 minutes in each direction. It was always an inconvenience whenever we had to head back, but tonight? That time, it seemed like five minutes. We were only a few minutes into our tour of the apartment when I looked over at Melinda, who was beaming. "This place is..." "Perfect," I finished for her. We've been finishing each other's sentences for over 20 years. Why stop now?

It wasn't the interior and its abundance of natural light, or the hardwood floors and the fancy stone countertops. It wasn't even the ingenious storage options built into the walls — though that, admittedly, made me geek out a bit. No, it was how this tiny space felt to us. It felt like home. We'd only been looking for a few weeks and just like that, we knew the search was over.

We took measurements, put down a deposit, settled on a move-in date, and went our separate ways, the landlord happy and us pinching ourselves for all our good fortune. Keeping the dimensions of our future home in mind, we spent the remainder of August paring down the rest of our earthly belongings even further. We got rid of a lot of furniture, purchasing replacements that utilized space more wisely. We digitized our CDs and DVDs. More painfully, we got rid of the bulk of our book collection, keeping a few treasured copies and buying in digital form the ones we knew we'd re-read down the road.

By the time moving day arrived, we'd slimmed down 20-plus years of memories into a 15-foot U-Haul. Our hard work had paid off in the intended way, but it also paid off in some unexpected ones.

Rekindling and reconnecting

Being forced to go through all of our belongings affected us profoundly and unexpectedly. The simple act of severing a bond to something, by either giving it away or throwing it out, offers tribute and, sometimes, much-needed closure. The same went for everything we kept.

I can't tell you how many times I sat in the attic, sweating profusely in the Carolina August heat, smiling at old pictures, paging through forgotten journals, re-reading love letters that I had written in pencil to my now-wife when we were in high school, and later, college-era notes written in fountain pen. Some of it you keep; some of it you part with. In both cases, for better or worse, you reconnect with the life you've lived.

We've been in our tiny apartment for about six months now, and I can honestly say that we're the happiest we've ever been. I get immense comfort from being able to see everything we own from almost anywhere in our home. It all has a place when you live in tiny quarters, and you know exactly where everything is.

People often ask, "How do you get away from each other?" And while that always sounds overly harsh to me, when the walls close in (and they can), I head outside. Often, I sit in the park across the street, eyes closed, listening to the city breathe. When your home consists of one room and a bathroom to the side, it's your surroundings that fill that gap. A coffee shop becomes your living room; the library, your study. A co-working space becomes your office. You meet new people. You make new friends. I know more people in my community now than I ever knew during the years we spent in suburbia.

The simple act of severing a bond to something, by either giving it away or throwing it out, offers tribute and, sometimes, much-needed closure.

The space where we sleep, cook, and get our mail is smaller, but our home is bigger than it's ever been. I never thought I'd smile simply walking down a city block. But I do, frequently, when I walk home after a long day of work. I'm in the best shape of my life because I walk almost everywhere now. We rarely get in our car, visiting a gas station once a month. Our monthly utility bill is a fraction of what it was. We are surrounded by amazing art, live music, unbelievable food, different cultures, and different ideas.

The list is long, but the result is simple. By intentionally living smaller, our lives expanded so much.

Choose Your Character

Faced with change, an all-female indie dev team evolves to a higher form.

By BRIANNA WU

belong to an elite order, the technological Illuminati of game development. My spellbook is a 2011 MacBook Pro with dual SSDs and $7,000 worth of professional 3D software. I am consumed by an endless internal fire to transform my passions into practical, playable reality.

It's the third mission today: a story conference with my lead animator, Amanda. I'm exhausted. Level creation is now on my long list of job duties, taking on the work of someone I fired. It's just an average day leading an indie-game development team.

Amanda is my best employee, and a yin to my yang. She was a cheerleader and the president of her sorority, then spent a decade as a retail manager before she changed careers and went back for a degree in 3D animation. She has a calm, considered presence, a counterbalance to my relentless impulse to charge forward.

We finish discussing the storyboards and decide to book our voice actresses for another round of sessions. I think we're done, but just as I start to edge my way out of the conversation, she sits down. "I need to tell you something, Bri, because it's going to seriously affect you as my employer."

Appeared in
Issue 14,
April 11, 2013

Artwork by Giant Spacekat

Our game, *Revolution 60*, would not be coming together without Amanda. I've come to count on her, not just for her animation skills, but for her perspective. I brace for impact: she's moving, she's quitting, she's found another job.

"I'm pregnant," she says. I don't reply immediately, and I'll mull over my tepid response for weeks.

"Congratulations?"

Everyone brings their political agenda to the table when it comes to female characters in video games; everyone complains if the women don't match their particular vision.

The only way to win is not to play

ZNV

GKY

Like most professional game developers, I grew up in thrall of Nintendo and Sony. But unlike most who wind up in my field, I found the women in those games to be more than pretty faces. They were deeply aspirational figures. I grew up in Mississippi, but there was little I could relate to in the small-town worries of whose daughter was in which beauty pageant. *Final Fantasy*'s Terra, an *esper* raised by humans, had an internal conflict that rang fiercely true to me. Reality never stood a chance.

One Christmas, my mother gave me $1,000 to buy a PS1 Net Yaroze development kit. My deeply religious parents rarely understood my interests, but they always supported them financially. I became obsessed with uncovering the secrets of developing a game, trying to figure out how to bring the girls I had been drawing since I was eight into the digital worlds of Terra, Celes, and Rydia. Fifteen years later, my wildest dreams are becoming a reality.

I never set out to create an all-girl game development studio. Amanda was my first employee, but her résumé was initially tossed aside in favor of several male candidates. My husband had been helping sort through the hundreds of résumés and discarded it. By accident, I spotted it in the reject pile. Her clip reel showed a cheery girl leaping up, waving her hand with exuberant personality.

"We're making a game based on my art style," I said. "Don't you see how this is exactly the kind of animator we need?"

"It's pretty girly," he replied. "I guess I just don't get that stuff."

I don't blame my husband. His reaction was a milder and more polite form of the response I'd received when showing the first round of character designs to some of my friends:

"Why are they all white?" sneered a liberal friend of mine before launching into a 20-minute screed about how offended he was by the naked shower scene in *Heavy Rain*.

SRS

"I don't like playing games with women characters," said a conservative friend of mine. "Their sexuality is distracting. I don't need to see that!"

"Why doesn't the media show *my* body type?" demanded one girl. "I am *tired* of being the punch line. You can be overweight and healthy, and games like yours need to show that to our daughters."

"Why aren't any of the characters guys?" complained another. "Are you trying to say that women don't need men anymore?"

"They look anorexic," came one reaction.

Everyone brings their political agenda to the table when it comes to female characters in video games; everyone complains if the women don't match their particular vision. I start to wonder if the only way to win this game is not to have women at all.

Nega-Brianna

I'm late for a programming meeting with Maria, and don't have time to be stuck in Boston traffic. So instead of grabbing my car keys, I don black, skin-tight leather armor and leap onto my motorcycle. It's a 2009 Honda CBR600RR in racing red — something straight out of Akira. I've leaned into highway turns at 80 mph feeling nothing but speed, the air whipping all around me, and my thighs gripping a 212° F engine for dear life. My emotional connection to this 410 pounds of fuel and metal is intense.

HDM

Idling at a red light, I see a woman waiting to cross. She has my figure and looks to be my age. The frazzled look of motherhood is about her: disheveled hair and perpetual distraction. She's hunched over to hold the hands of two kids so beautiful that my heart gives an involuntary lurch — an instinct hardwired into my brain in ways I don't understand.

It hits me hard, as if this were an alternate-reality version of myself crossing the street. A Brianna that had made drastically different choices. The woman notices me. "Look at the girl on the motorcycle!" she says to her children. Our eyes meet. I recognize my gray-blue shade in her eyes.

I was adopted, and I had planned to do the same. But recently I've changed my mind. I wonder for the billionth time if the right decision is to concentrate on my job.

I'm certain that if I had children, I would be failing at my job.

I've hit my 30s, a period when it seems as if all of my friends suddenly have kids. That's a priority shift completely incompatible with my goals. Startups require that you give it all or go home, routinely requiring long nights, longer weekends, and blood and toil. If you aren't willing to put in the hours, eager replacements are standing behind you. If I fail, the women I work with will be out of their jobs.

The light turns red. I release the clutch and twist the throttle, and my doppelgänger and her children disappear in my wake.

A New Challenger appears

Maria's been working for us on weekends, but she spends her days as an administrative assistant at a radiation research company. She's my age, and brilliant at anything related to her job, but she might just feel less than brilliant outside of it. When we need the impossible to be possible, we send it to Maria.

With our next round of funding in hand, we set out to hire another full-time programmer. I ask Maria to sit in on the interview, as she has the right coding background (c++) to evaluate the candidate and will be working closely with him — all the applicants so far are male. Our potential hire has the easy confidence of a guy in his mid-20s. Better yet, he's personable, a rare trait among gamedev coders. He's our lead candidate. Maria is quieter than usual.

A few days later, Maria and I sit down to talk about her role over the next year. She's as introverted a person as I've ever known. Talking to her, you can sense the storm raging inside her mind, like she can't quite decide which lightning bolt to hurl. She manages to blurt, "I'd like to be considered for the lead programmer job."

"I've been wondering why you didn't apply."

"I didn't think I had enough experience," she stammers, "until I saw the résumés of people you were interviewing."

"ios Unreal is less than two years old." I say. "No one has experience with it yet."

Maria's managed to catch me off guard. I see so much of myself in her. If it were possible to reach into my chest and give her some of the fire that drives me, I would. I like our top outside pick, but I know I've got to bet on Maria. She's meant for so much more than answering phones.

"Can you start next month?"

Choose your Destiny

"I don't know if I can do this, Bri," says Amanda. It's the day after she told me she was pregnant. She's more scared than I've ever seen her, and she sounds like she's never felt more alone. She's been with her boyfriend for five years, longer than I've known my husband. She's worried what people will say. She's worried her parents will be disappointed in her.

I've loudly proclaimed my feminist principles from the rooftops for my entire life. But now those beliefs are in direct conflict with my responsibility to ship our game. Amanda is the linchpin of the company. I'm terrified I'm going to lose her, just as I have friends after they have had children and disappeared into the routine of family and schools.

"This is happening at the worst possible time. I'm 30, I just started my career over, and I'm worried if I stop now, I won't get another chance."

This is the real stuff of womanhood, not the video game fantasy we've spent so many hours creating. It's a gut check. What do you really want, Amanda? And what will you sacrifice to get it?

"I know all of that, and I'm terrified," she cries, "but having this baby is something I need to do."

I take a breath. In indie-game development you have to bet. Am I willing to bet my company on Amanda sticking with the project after she's become a mom?

"What do you need to make this happen?" I ask.

Paradigm Shift

I find myself reading academic articles on the psychology of introversion, trying to understand why the hell Maria and I can't stop butting heads. I'm an ENTJ, and she's an INTJ. Small difference; all the difference in the world.

We're having an all-hands meeting, and I'm doing all I can to not lose my temper. We have a major development deadline to hit, and it's one that's going

GMS

FRR

to require a lot of extra hours from Maria. I've spent the last week learning about one of her job functions in order to add my labor to hers. My intent is the height of altruism: I want to be the kind of leader that gets down in the trenches, not a desk jockey dispatching orders.

She is not pleased with changes I've proposed.

"You can't implement touch-to-move points," she says matter-of-factly. "You'd have to do it in Kismet and not UnrealScript, and that means the player can't look around with the camera."[1] It's the first of many of my ideas that will be shot down during this meeting.

I've come to understand that it's hard for Maria to collaborate without preparation. I like to talk through problems with people; she prefers to think through problems on her own. This does not make her instinctive "no" feel less irritating. Nor does the fact that I know she's right.

Afterward, I suggest Maria and I go get sandwiches to help smooth things over. Despite the headbutting, we've made tough, productive decisions. "You have to be proud of how much you've grown this year," I say. "I can't believe you used to work as a secretary."

"I was an administrative assistant, Bri," she corrects. "And it was part of a huge leap for me! Did you know I saved money for two years to come here and go to school? There were so many times I thought, 'Crap, I owe a lot of money!' But it was the first step on this road."

She's usually not this talkative. You have to coax her out of her shell. My gut instinct for direct communication has been completely wrong. "Do you feel like us giving you this job helped you grow past your shyness?" I ask.

"Our relationship sometimes gets tense because of our personality differences, but it's forced me to be more flexible," she says. Maria takes a breath. "Bri, I was talking to my brother," she says. "And I feel like I've earned a portion of our sales as a bonus after we ship. I've earned it."

And just that quickly, the emotional shield comes up and I have to retreat back into boss mode. But behind that shield, there's a smile. I know that the shy Maria I met a year ago never would have had the guts to bring this up.

The journey is the reward

Other gamedev companies have Christmas parties, and after two years of working together I've decided we need one too. The big attraction is a *Mario Kart 64* tournament. A $100 bill is waiting on the TV, bounty for the winner.

We've brought a game designer, Jenna, onto the team as a contractor. She's recently gone freelance after leaving her job at a major Boston game developer. She and her fiancé are curled up on the floor, awaiting their turn.

"I've really enjoyed working with you," says Jenna. "I've never had a work environment like this. I feel like my ideas are really respected, and I haven't felt a second of politics."

I just smile. In the last year, I've learned to conduct meetings while a baby causes blind, screaming chaos. And I've learned not to leap feet-first into every problem with Maria. Giving Jenna a little room is no problem.

The evening turns to the centerpiece, the *Mario Kart* tournament. Jenna has just smoked my husband, ensuring her place in the finals. The next numbers are drawn from the lottery. "It's Maria versus...Brianna!"

"Oh god," mutters Amanda.

A look of intense determination flashes in Maria's eyes. Boss or not, she's playing to win. And though she's been quiet most of the evening, an easy smile is on her face. She's colored her hair bright red, and Nintendo cartridge earrings playfully dangle from her ears. She almost didn't make it to our party because of the boardgame club where she's been spending her weekends.[2]

Amanda's daughter, Emma, crawls into the room. "Oh, I have the best Christmas present for her!" I say, passing Amanda a wrapped present. "I saw this on Amazon, and I just had to buy it for her."

"What's this?" says Amanda to Emma, reaching into the bag and gasping. "It's a puppet of Elmo!" Emma's face lights up, and she lets out a squeal of joy, recognizing the smiling red face of her favorite *Sesame Street* character. Amanda wiggles her fingers, and Elmo gives Emma a giant hug.

The first time I met Emma, Amanda asked me if I wanted to hold her. I was terrified I would break her. I'd never touched anything that seemed so simultaneously small yet heavy. Emma stared at me so intently I started to feel uncomfortable. There was a quizzical look on her face, as if she couldn't quite figure me out.

Last week, Amanda and I were musing over coffee. "I needed to have Emma," she said, "but the thought of losing my identity kept me up at night. That's why I work so hard on *Revolution 60*. It's how I keep 'me.'"

I think back to my lukewarm response a year earlier and how much we've accomplished since. We're right on track to deliver a killer game. "You didn't lose yourself at all," I replied. "You're more tired, sometimes a bit scattered, but you consistently kick ass." It was harder for me to speak aloud my next thought. "It makes me wonder if I made the right decision," I admit. "Because you showed me it can be done."

There's a long pause. Amanda said, "For right now, we're both doing exactly what we need to be doing."

At the party, I watch Amanda as she plays with her daughter, studying the way she interacts with Emma. It comes so naturally to her. This silly language she has with her daughter is not one that I speak. But now it doesn't seem as intimidating as it once did.

"Can I try?" I ask, reaching for the puppet.

Afterword *In the year since this article was printed, Giant Spacekat has grown, and it's closer to finishing* Revolution 60 *than ever. Amanda gave up on trying to work with a toddler in the house, bit the bullet, and enrolled her daughter in daycare. Now, Emma runs wild under supervision and her mom animates in peace. Maria is more comfortable than ever in her role as lead engineer and is preparing to train a junior software engineer for the sequel. We've also added two new people to our studio: Emma (an adult Emma, which will surely cause no confusion) and Carolyn.*

As for me? After this article went to print, I received a slew of professional speaking invitations, including giving the keynote for i360. I have five more scheduled for 2014. I feel, for now, that commanding a gamedev studio and being a voice for women in the industry is my first, best destiny. Revolution 60 *ships in a mere 58 workdays from when I write this.*

---

1 The heart of our game is the Unreal Engine, which has multiple ways to build out gameplay. Kismet nodes are essentially visual representations of self-contained blocks of UnrealScript or native (C++) code. It is ideal for quick prototyping, as well as for one-off events that occur in a specific game level. However, aside from being slower to execute, Kismet limits a programmer to functions that come with the engine. With UnrealScript, we can add more-efficient, game-wide features.

2 For the record, I won. Which is a little awkward, since that was my $100 we were fighting for. In the spirit of collaboration and the holidays, I split it three ways as an extra holiday bonus among Maria, Amanda, and Jenna.

Strange Game

Journey's lessons can apply to all of human endeavor.

By JOHN SIRACUSA

J*ourney* for the PlayStation 3 is the best video game I've played in a long
time. I'm going to use it to illustrate a larger point about technology, and
in doing so, I'm going to spoil the game. If you have any interest in video
games at all, I strongly recommend that you do not read any further
until you've played it.

Online discourse can be harsh. Nowhere is this more true than in multiplayer video games. It's nearly impossible to play a popular online game without
being exposed to — or worse, being the target of — the most vile kinds of behav-
iors and insults, including sexist, racist, and homophobic slurs.

This problem is not confined to video games. Even something as seemingly
benign as a comment form on a popular technology blog can trigger profoundly
bad behavior. A well-known *Penny Arcade* comic sums up the phenomenon
nicely in the form of John Gabriel's Greater Internet F—wad Theory, which
states: Normal Person + Anonymity + Audience = Total F—wad.

Many remedies have been tried: moderation, the use of "real names" (whatever that means), increasingly complex privacy settings, user voting, karma

STR

HWD

WHS

scores, and so on. Sometimes these things help, but often only a little — and they all require constant vigilance.

In frustration, many users and content creators choose to take out the big hammer and end discourse entirely. Eliminate blog comments. Mute all voice chat. Disable communication between players on opposing teams. The only winning move is not to play.

GLP

DLB

In Journey, *players inevitably find themselves having positive interactions with others.*

So goes the conventional wisdom. But then there's *Journey*, a $15 video game for the PlayStation 3. When you start playing *Journey*, it's not even obvious that it's a multiplayer game. When other players appear, they are not announced in any way, nor are you directed to interact with them. Some players choose to ignore them and complete the game on their own. Others dismiss them as computer-controlled NPCs. This is the first part of *Journey*'s solution: interaction with others is optional.

YRL

Those who choose to engage with others have only a few choices. Players can move, jump, and "sing" by pressing a single button, causing a musical note to play and a unique glyph to appear onscreen. The glyph is not selected or drawn by the player; it's automatically chosen by the game (so penis-themed griefing is out of the question). There is no text or voice chat. Singing is the only way to communicate, and the only control the player has over the note that's played is the volume and duration.

XJB

Most critically, none of these actions can harm other players. Even movement can't be used as a weapon; players simply pass through each other, making it impossible to bump other players off a high ledge or otherwise perturb their progress. Movement can't even be used to race ahead and steal a desirable in-game item before another player can get to it, because power-ups are not consumed when acquired; they remain in place for future players to receive.

PPF

All of this may sound like it stops just short of banning communication entirely. Will players even bother to interact with each other? Surely such a limited palette of options will render the multiplayer aspects of *Journey* trite and inconsequential.

 Type http://magcode.me/ plus a blue code in the margin to visit the related Web page.

But that's not what happens at all. Instead, *Journey* players find themselves having some of the most meaningful and emotionally engaging multiplayer experiences of their lives. How is this possible?

Though players can't harm each other, they can *help* each other. Touching another player recharges the power used to leap and (eventually) fly. In cold weather, touching warms both players, fighting back the encroaching frost. More-experienced players can guide new players to secret areas and help them through difficult parts of the game.

Journey players are not better people than *Call of Duty* players or *Halo* players. In fact, they're often the same people. The difference is in the design of the game itself. By so thoroughly eliminating all forms of negative interaction, all that remains is the positive.

Players do want to interact; real people are much more interesting than computerized entities. In *Journey*, players inevitably find themselves having positive interactions with others. And as it turns out, many people find these positive, cooperative interactions even more rewarding than their usual adversarial gaming experiences.

Does this mean that playing *Journey* turns players into relaxed, peace-loving, spiritually enlightened beings? Certainly not — but the limited communication system works in more ways than one.

In the same way that you can imagine that all the actors in a subtitled film (speaking in a language you don't understand) are giving Oscar-worthy performances, it's natural to assume that every other *Journey* player has only the best intentions. After all, while we may judge ourselves by our motivations, we tend to judge others by their actions. The actions in *Journey* are all either neutral or positive, so that's how players perceive each other.

Journey players are also anonymous during the game. The unique player glyphs are only shown next to PlayStation Network account names when the game is over, and they change on each play-through. Again, this plays into that subtitled-movie optimism. It's much easier to believe that the anonymous player with the winged glyph is the most caring, thoughtful person in the world when you don't know that his PSN account name is K1LLsh0t99.

If you want some evidence of the deep feelings triggered by this game, look no further than the *Journey* Apologies thread in the official forum for the game. Here, players apologize to the anonymous others they feel they have disappointed in the game. It's like missed connections for gamers. Here's an example post:

♦♦♦

Appeared in
Issue 2,
Oct. 25, 2012

ZTR

SXJ

KQB

To my friend in the fifth area: I never wanted to leave you. I just whiffed really badly
on a jump. I miss you. And I'm sorry.

Journey may be just a game, but the lessons it teaches us about ourselves
and the things we're capable of creating can be applied to all of human endeavor.

Throughout history, we humans have invented many different sets of rules
for ourselves. Some have worked better than others, but all of them have been
exploited. As anyone with children knows, if there's one thing humans are good
at, it's finding loopholes.

When a system of rules is applied to many people, thoroughly codified, and
consistently enforced, you have something approaching a government. But for
governments, even the most successful change occurs slowly and often painfully). This can lead even the most optimistic person to despair.

Human history is long, but how many different sets of rules have really been
tried? In meatspace, it's so difficult to establish a new set of rules or change the
existing ones that the rate of design iteration is severely limited.

This is not so in the relatively consequence-free worlds of video games and
the Internet. In the digital realm, wild experimentation and rapid iteration are
the norm. It's also much easier to establish and enforce an ironclad set of rules
in a virtual world than in the real one. This is the environment that created *Journey*, and its rarity is why it's such a joy.

The lesson of *Journey* is that success is possible, even in an area like online
multiplayer interaction, which has seemed so hopeless for so long over so many
thousands of iterations. Success is possible.

But let's go further. Our digital lives increasingly affect our real lives. Consider Twitter, another system for online interaction that has succeeded in large
part thanks to its novel set of rules and limitations. There's a whole world of bad
behavior that doesn't fit into 140 characters and doesn't work when producer/
consumer relationships are asymmetrical. Twitter isn't just a game; its influence
extends into the real world, in ways we don't yet fully understand.

As another US presidential election season grinds on and I become freshly
disillusioned with the seemingly intractable problems in our system of government, *Journey* and Twitter give me hope. They make me believe that maybe, just
maybe, the digital world can be both a laboratory for new ideas and, eventually,
a giant lever with which to change the formerly unchangeable.

ZWX

DRD

Roll for Initiative

I cast a spell of +10 confidence.

By SCOTT MCNULTY

Appeared in
Issue 14,
April 11, 2013

D espite the complete darkness, I sensed where I was: standing on the edge of a crevasse deep underground. I felt the rough rock under my hands as I waited for my friends to finish crossing. Then I spotted him. He was a member of the party, our paladin — and also my target.

Slowly I loaded the poisoned bolt into the hand crossbow I kept at my side for just such an occasion. The lack of light was no obstacle for an archer of my talent; the bolt flew steady and true. It slid through a gap in his plate armor with a satisfyingly meaty thwack. I knew the bolt wouldn't kill him, but I hoped the poison would.

You'll shoot your eye out, kid

I held the BB gun tightly in my hands as I stood in the tiny backyard of Kevin's house. I had never fired a BB gun, but Glenn assured me that it was easy. I had met Glenn only 10 minutes earlier, and now I was taking firearms advice from him. I pumped the gun a couple of times to fill its chamber with air, took aim, and completely missed the flower that was our mutual target.

Shooting daffodils in a backyard wasn't a normal activity for me, especially not with someone I had just met, but our mutual friend Kevin had convinced us to start playing some game called Dungeons & Dragons — D&D for short.[1] We were outside while Kevin was busily creating a character with another one of my friends.

I was 12 years old, and talking to new people filled me with dread. It didn't come naturally, so I needed a hook. Hence, there we stood shooting flowers and getting to know one another.

With nary a second thought I jump down the serpent's gullet and manage to survive long enough to say the words to my spell. I hope the cleric remembers me fondly.

Now Glenn is one of my closest friends. Whenever we talk, we pick up as if our conversation on that day almost 25 years ago had never ended.[2]

D&D made that friendship possible, and it also equipped me with the tools to handle just about any social situation without an overwhelming sense of impending doom, or at least slight social anxiety.

Character-forming experiences

Dungeons & Dragons is a roleplaying game; in fact, it wouldn't be an exaggeration to call it *the* roleplaying game. All that's required to play the game is a couple of rulebooks, some pens, paper, dice, a few friends, and a lot of imagination.[3]

The books contain the set of rules that the Dungeon Master (DM for short) applies to the world he or she creates. The DM is god — all the gods in fact. The DM runs everything in the world, with one critical exception: the player characters (PCs) who are the heroes or villains of the adventure. Each person gathered around the table takes the part of a player character. The characters themselves are much like those from a play or television show, formed within the rubric of the D&D rules by input from the player, the DM, and chance.

Player characteristics — known in-game as stats — like wisdom, intelligence, and dexterity are traditionally assigned scores based on the roll of three six-sided dice. Characters are granted powers and abilities from the combination of a class (cleric, fighter, magic user, and so on) and a race. All your favorite fantasy races are accounted for, as well as some that you've never heard of unless you're a D&D player. (I'm partial to tieflings myself.)[4] Each player takes a character and roleplays as it, reacting to situations as the character would.

While a character is just a piece of paper with some writing on it, roleplaying makes it live. The best roleplayers breathe life into their characters and make them their own. The character becomes an extension of the player.

Leaping leviathan

The waves toss the ship under my feet and I struggle to grab onto the railing to avoid falling into the water, which would mean almost certain death. The gigantic sea monster had come from nowhere and attacked the ship. We're all just trying to stay out of the water when it happens: the monster swallows our cleric whole. There's no way that he'll survive for long in that monster's belly.

I muster up my most explosive spell from memory and go about getting to the one place it'll do the most damage in the quickest way: the belly of the beast. With nary a second thought I jump down the serpent's gullet and manage to survive long enough to say the words to my spell.

I hope the cleric remembers me fondly.

Talk amongst yourselves

I had no idea what I was getting myself into that afternoon as I made my character with Kevin. I didn't know I would return to his house every Friday night for the next six years and gather around his decidedly non-ergonomic coffee table with a group of guys whose ages ranged from 16 to 30-something (which seemed very old to me then) to adventure for fame and fortune, with an emphasis on the fortune.

I soon found that the common goal of the group within the game gave an introvert like me something to talk about no matter the differences in age or experience between myself and the other players. The very nature of the game also helped me feel more at ease interacting; everyone has a specific turn in which they state their actions.

Applying this structure to something that is usually unstructured (that is, the real world) gives you time to think and an obvious cue to speak. Despite that, the most enjoyable games I've played in have included healthy doses of tangential banter.

Twenty-sided die! Die! Die!

Playing a character frees me to say and do things that the real me would never consider, like shooting a friend of mine in the side with a poisoned bolt while underground. I would never go spelunking.

My most successful characters reflect and magnify parts of my own personality. They also tend to be incredibly evil or annoyingly good. (Anyone who has played in a group with a by-the-book paladin knows what I'm talking about, and I only play the strictest stick-in-the-mud paladins.)[5]

Unshackling myself from doubt in the game allows me to open up and take charge of situations. In my day-to-day life, I tend to measure my words for a long time before speaking. I overthink almost every one of my actions to comedic lengths. Loric, the happy fellow who shot that poisoned bolt, doesn't suffer from such meddlesome restraints. As a blind Drow elf archer (really), Loric answers most questions quickly and with the same response: an arrow to a vital organ.

I don't ask myself "What would Loric do" when I'm in social situations — answer: whatever he wanted — but I do try to disengage my various anxieties and be in the moment, as Loric always is.

Six seals' sick sin

The chamber we've returned to contains the six broken seals. Seals that weren't broken until we visited them the first time. Having traveled across six dimensional planes, we've recovered the pieces of an artifact to repair the damage to the six seals holding back the legions of hell from our reality.

I hold the completed artifact in my hands. Because I am the only character in our group who has any arcane ability and knowledge, it falls to me to activate the artifact and repair the seals. That's what I've promised the group that I would do. There's a slight problem: I sold my soul to the devil years ago, and the devil has other plans.

As the group battles a variety of monsters to protect me, I complete the complicated magic required — not to repair the seals, but rather to siphon their power into me. I feel a twinge of regret. Maybe I should do what I promised? Nah, I need to rule in hell, and this is the only way to do that. Besides, I won't kill any of my friends...if I can avoid it.

Fantasy league

Despite the fact that my characters often do horrible things, I've made a number of good friends at the D&D table. When I moved to Philadelphia 10 years ago, I didn't know anyone. Chances are my social circle would be much smaller if I hadn't found a welcoming D&D group that I still play with.

My current gaming group has changed configurations and locations since I joined, but one thing remains the same: every Friday night we slip out of our regular lives and don armor to battle evil together. It is a surprisingly effective way to get to know people. The players around the table range from devout Christians to radical atheists, college students to professors, and extroverts to the shy, but we are all friends because we pretend to be elves together.

Applying the lessons I've learned from D&D to my life has made me a little less introverted. With cues taken from my various characters, I've created something of an alternate Scott McNulty to play when interacting in social situations. Social Scott is very much like Real Scott, except that he makes an effort to engage in conversation and doesn't spend the entire time he is at a party thinking about books.

Social Scott isn't a hero or villain, but he does let me accrue valuable experiences — life points? — that would normally pass me by. Most importantly, Social Scott makes Real Scott a better and more believable character.

---

1 Dungeons & Dragons has gone through a number of revisions, with a bewildering array of source material available for it. I've played games in all of the major editions, as well as some of the board games.

2 The Glenn in question is not the editor of this fine publication.

3 D&D makes use of a variety of dice. The traditional six-sided die is joined by those with 4, 8, 10, 12, and 20 sides, to name a few. In fact, the 20-sided die is the most iconic random generator used in the game.

4 Tieflings are demonic-looking humanoids who are generally thought to have made a deal with a demon in some bygone era. In the 4th edition of Dungeons & Dragons, they are available as a playable race.

5 Think of a paladin as the White Knight. He's a holy warrior concerned with protecting the weak and righting wrongs.

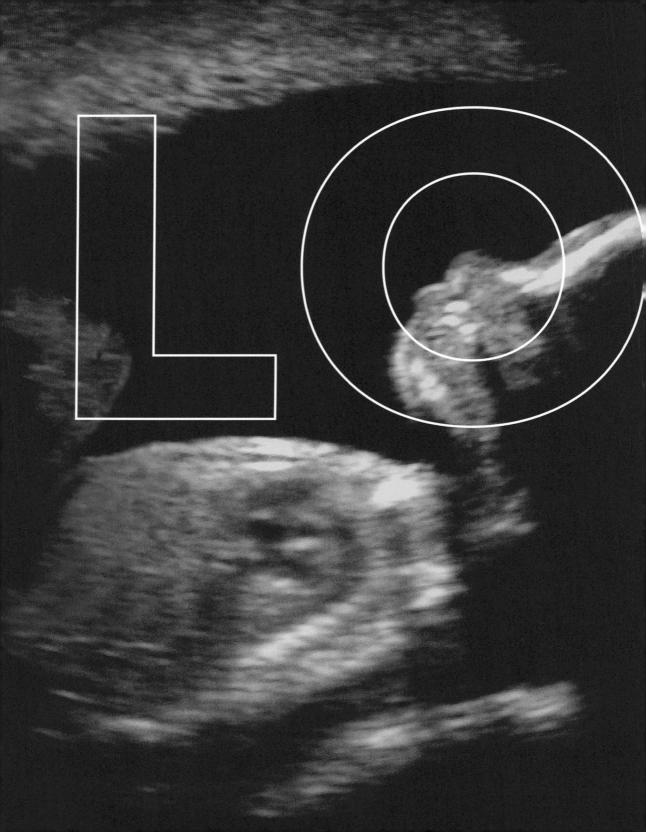

OK

WITHIN

We can be responsible for machines.

By LISA SCHMEISER

Reproduction is one of the few commonalities across human cultures. Take that away and you have the Shakers. This underscores two sad truths: without reproduction, your culture doesn't thrive; and children and nice furniture are fundamentally incompatible.

By its very nature, pregnancy should be one of those universal human experiences, like eating a piece of fruit you've just picked or smelling the ozone and petrichor that accompany a good hard rain. Yet speaking as someone who was pregnant in the recent past, I found how much it had changed since my mother bore me. For one, she couldn't post a belly-shot montage on YouTube.

Back in grad school, where we sat around and pondered vague and important-sounding questions about how technology would disrupt the definitions of society — in my defense, it was the 1990s, and everyone who was anyone was reading the deconstructionists — we read "A Cyborg Manifesto," by Donna Haraway. The essay is a cri de coeur for the rejection of identity politics, and Haraway uses the metaphor of the cyborg to make the argument for people becoming comfortable playing with questions of personal and social identity.

As I dealt with the technological double whammies of Western prenatal care, with its scans and tests, and the everyday use of what Haraway would probably call a "polymorphous information system" but what we would call "the Internet," I felt very cyborg indeed.

Perhaps unsurprisingly, the technological elements of pregnancy — both the ones introduced through social interactions (Facebook and beyond) and the ones I encountered at the doctor's office — were the things that left me feeling most alienated, from both myself and my culture at large.

A pregnant pause

Although people like to view pregnancy as a binary state — you either are or you are not — it is also a deeply liminal one. For 40 weeks, you're suspended between two separate family configurations. Your family isn't what it used to be, but it's not what it's going to be. You're not who you were, but you're not what you're going to be. You're drifting between borders.

Liminal states can be unsettling, and people cope with the unease in a variety of ways. A lot of my fellow preggos made a determined effort to package their pregnancy for public commodification, as if determining a narrative would somehow eliminate any of the borderlands of ambiguity ringing the daily realization that everything in your life is going to shift and rearrange in unimaginable patterns.

At least, this was my charitable explanation for the explosion of "adorable" staged photos announcing someone's pregnancy or the gender of their child; for the profusion of nursery makeover posts I saw on Facebook; for the vicious message board brawls I witnessed as grown women stressed over what to pack in their hospital bags. As people chewed over the minutiae of pending parenthood, I would read posts from friends and strangers and wonder why I couldn't relate.

My pregnancy was a long slog through a no-woman's land to enter at last

We are living through a movement from an organic, industrial society to a polymorphous, information system. — HARAWAY

into a wholly undiscovered country. No amount of nursery decorating or posting milestones on my Facebook timeline could prepare me for what lay ahead. Pretending I knew what I was getting into would seem to push me away from my real self, whoever she still was.

I coped with my alienation by re-reading a lot of sci-fi that treated the intersection of technology and pregnancy as a horror show — "Bloodchild," by Octavia Butler; *The Handmaid's Tale*, by Margaret Atwood; and *Dr. Pak's Preschool* and *Piecework*, by David Brin. Somehow, reading about pregnancies that turned into nightmares via invasive, dignity-stripping technology made me feel better about my own Facebook-induced agita.

DFW

YRR, JXS

JLB

Arranged in order of size

If you are a middle-class pregnant female in North America in the early 21st century, you will likely find yourself at any one of a number of Web sites aimed at expectant parents, all of which offer weekly email newsletters which will tell you what's going on in your body as the pregnancy progresses.

I signed up for two of these newsletters. And every week, I read that "your baby" — never a fetus, always "your baby" — was the size of a poppy seed, a sesame seed, a peppercorn, a nutmeg. Once I hit the second trimester, we left the spice drawer and moved into the crisper: a Persian cucumber, a mango, a small summer squash, etc.

I unsubscribed from one newsletter the week that I learned I was carrying the equivalent of "two heirloom tomatoes." I refuse to let any editor think it's

acceptable to draw a direct line between slow food and slow gestation.

The specificity of the emails made me worry that my cohort and I would be relentlessly factual in our pregnancies. What would we talk about — how our blood volume had increased by 30 to 50 percent?

Thankfully, no. We talked about the emails. "Are you getting the food comparisons?" was the first thing someone would say. The second was, "What was the food item that made you snap?" For my friend Maria, it was a cheese-covered mango. "Who does that? Why would you cover a mango in cheese? Why not just use a burrito?"

Finding kindred spirits to wax wroth about fetus-as-food comparisons provided one of the few moments where I felt a graceful integration of the cultural aspects of pregnancy and the technological tools that had sprung up to service and supplement the culture.

I need not have worried that I was finally easing into some serenely networked Mother Earth role. There were still plenty of liminal spaces left.

Echoes in the depths

Many parts of being pregnant remind you that you aren't the first to bear a child; you are linked through physical sensation to every mother who came before you. The strongest twinges can knock you into the pleasantly dislocated feeling of being adrift on a river out of time. Oh, your left hip is doing that thing where every step you take causes an exquisite, narrow lance of pain from pelvis to ankle? I bet some poor pioneer woman felt that when she was walking beside the covered wagon.

Appeared in
Issue 24,
Aug. 29, 2013

There is nothing about being "female" that naturally binds women. There is not even such a state as "being" female, itself a highly complex category constructed in contested sexual scientific discourses and other social practices. — HARAWAY

Still, the pioneer women didn't have the pressure of feigning maternal feelings at the 12-week fetal scan. Because I was what the doctor's office charmingly termed "elderly primagravida" — and because I had spent the first month of my pregnancy, before I was aware I was enceinte, marinating in hot tubs, drinking a lot of very good French wine, and eating a lot of mercury-laden shiro maguro — I had an ultrasound so that we could manage everyone's expectations.

The screen was filled with what looked like a Rorschach test. I squinted as the technician pointed out the blobs that were presumably the fetus's working kidneys, hummingbird-fast heart, and rapidly developing brain. I feel like I should have been thrilled by this proof that cell division and differentiation were ticking along.

But I was more bowled over by the notion that someone, somewhere had said, "What if we assigned a visual representation to the mathematical distance calculated by the speed of sound and the time of that sound's echoing return? Wouldn't that be cool to see off what that sound bounced?" The notion of taking

one set of physical measurements to find something new and undiscovered —
much like archaeologists are doing in Honduras with LIDAR — is breathtaking. A
weird blob that lives in your torso with bits and pieces occasionally pulsing? Eh.

Going by the prevailing rhetoric on my birth board and among my friends, I
was an outlier. The majority of people who gazed upon their little Oort clouds
had crossed some cognitive and emotional chasm. Not only were these women
carrying babies, they were already calling themselves mothers, and all of their
acts and thoughts seemed to be motivated by some gush of motherly love.

Eh, I thought again. There's always the 21-week scan.

We are all chimeras, theorized and fabricated hybrids of machine and organism; in short, we are cyborgs. — HARAWAY

Alas, my 21-week appointment also failed to fill me with the rush of trans-
formative maternal wonder. I had visited my friend and fellow preggo Maria
shortly before, and she had had her 20-week ultrasound framed. In it, the sil-
houette of a snub-nosed baby boy was clearly visible, exciting proof that Maria
was carrying an actual human baby. I was looking forward to my own adorable
photographic proof.

Part of the visit included genetic counseling, which I was partly looking forward to because the phrase "genetic counseling" suggests a tearful session
where recessive alleles sob, "I just want one chance to express myself!" while a
doctor holds up a warning hand and tells the dominant alleles, "You've already
had a chance to speak."

The reality was that a very nice woman got derailed when I asked where the
Punnett squares for all the genetic disease alleles were. She wanted us to be
relieved and grateful that neither of us was heterozygous dominant for any
heartbreaking hereditary conditions, and instead I was openly piqued I couldn't
see the PCR films that would have sequenced our DNA and showed the specific
markers on sequenced genes.

I had already opened an entire condiment tray's worth of emails telling me
the average fetus's probable size for the week. What I wanted was to know what
was written in this specific fetus's genome. We had the technology; why weren't

we using it? I may as well be back with all my relatives, clucking about someone with, "You know she's having a girl? Girls steal all their mother's beauty and she's looked terrible since she started to show."

My husband defused my snit. "There, there. Soon you're going to be speared with a harpoon for science."

Prepare to be boarded

"I'm really looking forward to my amniocentesis procedure" is not a phrase commonly uttered during pregnancy — mostly because nobody says, "I am eagerly anticipating the moment when someone jams a 20-gauge needle into an internal organ" — but I really was looking forward to it.

I've always been fascinated by what lies underneath my skin. I was excited to see some of this amniotic fluid, since I didn't remember my first exposure to it. And I was even more excited by the prospect that we'd find out even more medical markers for our pending child.

My husband has a mild needle aversion, so he did not share my fascination. "Oh, don't worry," I reassured him. "The needle's so big, it has to be wheeled in. The beeping of the forklift will warn you it's coming."

Getting amnio was really no big thing. You don't even feel the needle — there's a local anesthetic to numb the area — and then there you are, watching it fill with a slightly cloudy golden liquid, which the technician assured us was that color because the baby was peeing in it.

And off went our baby's pee — and other liquid substances — to be analyzed for signs of any chromosomal problems that the genetic counseling panel had missed, plus other nightmares like metabolic disorders or neural tube defects. I sourly thought, There goes another data set I'll never see.

Then we moved on to the ultrasound. I took my husband's hand in preparation for what surely would be one of the most tender moments of our life together...

...And saw the nightmare crest of a Viking battle helmet. The fetus elected to give us a full frontal shot, so what we saw — grinning skull with outsized cranial cavity and hollow eye sockets; spindly, claw-like appendages; disturbingly sharp ribs — was suitable for framing only if the proud papa were H.R. Giger.

Phil and I both reared back. The technician gave us a look that suggested we were already terrible parents. "Is baby's spine," she said in a Russian accent that her years in America hadn't worn down. We could see every mace-shaped vertebra floating below that grinning death's-head noggin. "Is baby's heart. Looks good. Is baby's kidneys. Looks good. Baby has toes" — they looked more like velociraptor claws, really — "baby's brain."

"So we see," we murmured. Part of my brain was hissing that I needed to be grateful for all the good news, that this was infinitely superior to spending an entire pregnancy hoping for the best but knowing nothing. The other part of my brain was musing that sometimes, technology lets us push the "I can do it!" button while completely ignoring the "Should I do it?" button.

"You want to know sex?" the technician asked. I shrugged and pressed the "I can do it!" button.

"No penis. Is girl."

This was something I could see, as opposed to some third-party pronouncement I was expected to swallow without question. So I was going to have an alien queen. I hoped she wouldn't ram her spike-like ovipositor down my throat the first time I tried to ground her.

The technician printed out a set of ultrasound prints, suitable for framing and giving to people upon whom you wished permanent psychological damage. We debated for only a moment before concluding that throwing the prints out would not make us bad parents.

When I went online after the Alien Queen reveal, I was saddened but unsurprised to discover that my cohort had all had photogenic ultrasounds: lots of adorably snub-nosed fetuses in profile, waving tiny hands at nothing in particular but captioned with things like, "Baby girl saying hi to her mama!"

I had seen my fetus's skeletal system and working organs and been reassured that all her chromosomes were in order. That still didn't make her feel any more like "baby girl." She was an organic data set, forever expanding with new parameters to query weekly. All the medical data in the world didn't change a fundamental truth of pregnancy: I was incubating a stranger.

Cyborgs have more to do with regeneration and are suspicious of the reproductive matrix and of most birthing. — HARAWAY

A familiar place

In the end, I had a scheduled C-section. A combination of data sets — my physiological measurements plus the fetus's measurements — led my obstetrician to suggest it, and I liked the idea of knowing exactly when this damned liminal state would end.

So one sunny, warm Monday afternoon, I waddled into the admissions area while my husband was parking the car, got prepped for surgery, and killed time reading on my Kindle until it was time for me to go have a baby.

I was wheeled into the operating room. The anesthesiologist gave me the lumbar puncture that made me numb from the mid-chest down, two nurses erected the please-don't-faint drape, and a pregnancy that had been remarkably transparent in terms of raw data ended with a delivery shrouded in mystery.

From my end, it felt like a bunch of people playing rugby, with my gravid form as the ball. I was rocked back and forth. There was a mighty pull, a shift of pressure right around my center of gravity, a high blatting sound, a shift in my brain. That was my baby, and she was crying.

My OB held up the baby, and I lifted my head. She was pink and round and had a lot of hair — the old wives were on to something with the heartburn. My baby was crying, and despite the fact that I was currently strapped to an operating table and gutted like a trout, I tried to get up and get to my daughter.

I said, "My baby needs me. I'm the only one she knows."

We can be responsible for machines; they do not dominate or threaten us. We are responsible for boundaries; we are they. — HARAWAY

It took minutes to wash, weigh, and swaddle her. I made Phil go hover next to the nurses, saying, "The baby can't be alone!" because apparently nurses didn't count as company. Someone somewhere was saying something about there being too much blood, about the bleeding not being under control.

Despite being the only person in the room who was likely to be bleeding, I could not have cared less — all of my attention was focused on listening to my daughter's furious shrills, and I kept saying, "I have to see her. She needs to be skin-to-skin, it will soothe her."

In an operating room, as people sloshed through great pools of blood, I rose above on a surging wave of maternal love. The tiny, spectator part of my brain marveled at how easily I fell into one of the biggest myths about motherhood, the one where you instantly love your child. But I did love this baby the minute I saw her as a baby. And I felt like her mother.

Just like that, the liminal stage was over.

Just Desert

Africa, a devil, and Burning Man meet in Eastern Europe's little desert.

By COLLEEN HUBBARD

With its brick-and-stone houses painted in muted rust tones, the small village of Chechło is typical of this region of southern Poland. The streets are empty save for the lunch rush at a cafeteria-style restaurant where scoops of steam-table chicken, potatoes, and cabbage land on industrial white plates.

As in most of Poland, the population in this region is dropping and graying: entry into the European Union in 2004 coupled with the easing of immigration standards among some member states meant that many of Poland's young people left to pursue educational and occupational opportunities elsewhere. From 2004 to 2011, the country's population decreased by one million people.

Yet Chechło's town green offers a sight that distinguishes it from surrounding hamlets, with their renovated farmhouses and gated gardens. Between a shrine of the Virgin Mary and a silver-blue fir tree, a statue of a Bactrian camel glares at an empty bus stop across the street. The camel's peach lips curl into a snarl, and time and sunshine have conspired to drain the color from patches of fur on his humps. His ear is another matter.

Appeared in
Issue 25,
Sept. 12, 2013

"Kids," shrugs Marian Pajdak, president of the Polish Sahara Association (PSA), gesturing at the hole that offers a view into the statue's hollow skull. Local teenagers are implicated in the crime of breaking off the camel's ear.

That Chechło is a one-camel town is not an accident. The village, and the surrounding region of Klucze, would like to bring your attention to an aberration of nature: a story of Nazis, Burning Man, Africa, pharaohs, silver mines, and, of course, moonshine.

It's the story of the Polish Sahara.

When we pass a local church, Pajdak points out that it's the building the devil hit. The steeple remains askew.

The devil, you say?

How a sort-of desert developed in Southern Poland depends on whom you ask. To start with, the Polish Sahara, called Pustynia Błędowska in Polish (Błędow Desert), is not really a desert.

Technically speaking, a desert is an area defined by aridity, though there is no universally accepted measurement or combination of measurements to define desert-level dryness, so the classification remains somewhat elastic. With rainfall typical for this region, along with an occasional choking fog, the Polish Sahara is only a desert insofar as Lake Michigan is an ocean if you've never left your mom's porch in Kenosha.

As to how the Błędow Desert appeared where it did, one story goes like this: In the Middle Ages, men discovered that the land here ran thick with silver and lead, so they began mining to extract it. Angry at the disruption to his subterranean home, a devil filled a bag with Baltic sand and raced back toward the open mines, intending to clog them and impede the miners' work. But as the devil sprinted across the low hills of Silesia, his bag of sand snagged on a church steeple, spilling the contents and creating the Błędow Desert.

Another version goes like this: In the 13th century, men discovered that the land in this area was rich in silver and lead. They stripped the local forest to power mining operations and construct mine shafts. After felling trees and hauling lumber out with horses, the destruction of native plant life was complete.

But underneath the pines, something unexpected materialized: a deep layer of sand deposited by a glacier that had dragged across this region.

Today, of course, no one believes the story of the angry devil protecting his home, but when we pass a local church, Pajdak points out that it's the building the devil hit. The steeple remains askew.

Up close with the exotic

As president of the PSA, Pajdak's role is to promote the educational, ecological, and cultural role of the desert in the region. He's a man of retirement age, with short silver hair in a slightly overgrown Caesar cut; he used to work as a journalist and teacher. Though he grew up in Wieliczka, near the salt mines south of Krakow, Pajdak's first desert wasn't the Błędow: he saw a desert when he traveled to West Africa with a contingent of journalists in the 1980s, and he visited Poland's desert for the first time 12 years after that.

Established 10 years ago with a name bestowed by a Jagiellonian University professor who resided in Chechło, the PSA emphasizes the Sahara-Africa connection in part to capitalize on interest in life outside of Poland among cosmopolitan young people from Krakow, who are the target market for the PSA's annual summer music festival in the desert.

Poland's small African Polish community has also played a role in defining and publicizing the Polish Sahara, says Dominik Mbeda Ndege, a musician whose Kenyan father and Polish mother met at a university in Poland. Mbeda Ndege is part of a Facebook group of about 600 young African Poles, and he recounted his visits to Ethiopia and South Africa on a Polish television show on which Poles who have traveled to far-flung locales offer an overview of their experiences with and the highlights of a foreign culture, including showing off knickknacks they acquired in their travels and demonstrating dance moves.

A black person in Poland remains an uncommon sight. After the murder,

displacement, and emigration of minorities during and following World War II, Poland became ethnically homogeneous: among the country's population of 38 million, only 1.4 percent claim to descend from an ancestry other than Polish. (That number includes those who self-identify as Kashubian or Silesian, ethnic groups from southern Poland.)

Only about 4,000 Poles living in Poland are black Africans, most of them living in the cities of Warsaw and Krakow. This small population hasn't stifled the Poles' fascination with the landscape, culture, and people of Africa, or African Poles' engagement with the local Polish community.

"It reminds me of home," Mbeda Ndege says while in the desert, looking at a crumbling bunker painted with images of black women wearing bright textiles and carrying baskets on their heads. "They're painted in an African style, not a European style."

The artist is Seydou Zan Diarra, a Mali-born small-animal veterinarian who lives in Krakow and lists the birthdays of his patients on his Web site, where in the "hobby" section he describes his interest in the art styles of the Dogon and Tuareg people of Africa. Mbeda Ndege, who plays tuba, and his brothers, who play trombone and saxophone, performed African and world music at the PSA's Desert Mirage festival in the Błędow. Photos and posters from the annual event show bare-chested white women wearing body paint and dancing in the center of a circle of onlookers.

The PSA also organizes and sponsors Africa-themed educational events in Krakow, including an exhibition of Seydou Zan Diarra's work, tastings of African foods, and screenings of documentaries and dramas filmed in Africa.

Mbeda Ndege, who plays tuba, and his brothers, who play trombone and saxophone, performed African and world music at the PSA's Desert Mirage festival in the Błędow.

Just add mortars and stir

When a little desert with dunes appeared in Eastern Europe, it proved lucky for many a tactician, of both the domestic and conquering varieties. In its early days, the desert had limited appeal for the community: locals found it creepy, and its commercial use was limited to the harvesting of the cochineal, a small insect that lives on the knawel plant and is crushed to create a crimson pigment called St. John's Blood.

Between World War I and World War II, the Kraków Army used the space as a training area. Ethnographer Marian Kantor-Mirski visited in the 1930s and in a monograph of regional history described the Błędow at that time as an "extensive emptiness, eerie wilderness, sea of sand."[1]

During World War II, the occupying German troops, including Field Marshal Erwin "Desert Fox" Rommel and his Afrikakorps, used the Błędow for tactical practice of maneuvers planned for the North African front. A propaganda photo passed off as an action shot from North Africa in fact depicts a Nazi soldier riding a motorbike on a dune in Poland.

After the close of World War II, the Polish army reestablished ownership

JNC
GZP

over the northern section of the desert. NATO carried out exercises there, and today the 6th Pomeranian Airborne Division uses the area as a paratrooper drop zone.

The Błędow, with its resemblance to a real desert (assuming one can't feel the temperature or see the fog), was also an easy choice for Polish filmmakers looking to take advantage of the dunes in their backyard as a low-cost film set.

Tad Makarczynski's 1962 allegorical short *Magician* (*Czarodziej*), about a wily sorcerer who turns a band of young boys into murderous soldiers by encouraging them to shoot increasingly realistic targets, appears to have been shot there.

Environmental pollution from Silesia speeded the regrowth: nitrogen runoff caused blue-green algae to develop, which in turn caused soil to take hold over the sand layer.

The land doubled as Egypt for scenes in the Polish production *Pharaoh* (*Faraon*), Jerzy Kawalerowicz's 1966 Oscar-nominated three-hour epic, in which a bunch of white guys dipped in bronze body paint squint meaningfully across ravaged vistas in a convoluted tale of Ancient Egyptian back-room politicking between Ramses XIII and a group of priests.

But the desert can't keep its secret, and the detritus from its use by the military still shows itself today, from crumbling concrete bunkers to spent mortar shells. Recently, sappers scoured the desert to locate and remove potentially dangerous military cast-offs. They even uncovered a half-ton dud. But long before experts arrived, during the Communist regime, villagers searched for shells to disassemble and sell as scrap metal.

"Especially in Chechło, there are people in their 70s and 80s who got their fingers blown off trying to disarm unexploded shells," Pajdak says.

When Magdalena Moroń, now deputy director of the Klucze district office, was a girl, kids playing in the desert planned treasure hunts for spent artillery shells and other military scrap.

"The kid who brought the most fun things home was the winner," she explains. "You couldn't call it an entirely safe way of playing."

Corrupting the natural

After the deforestation of the Middle Ages, the desert's area encompassed 150 square kilometers. Today, only 33 square kilometers of sand remain exposed. Over time, and with the reduction of mining and farming in Silesia and Małopolska, the desert was returning to its natural state.

Starting in the 1950s locals planted willows and firs in the area, hoping to avoid the regular afternoon chore of sweeping sand from their driveways and stoops. Environmental pollution from Silesia speeded the regrowth: nitrogen runoff caused blue-green algae to develop, which in turn caused soil to take hold over the sand layer. For some who lived near the Błędow, the disappearing desert seemed like a lost opportunity.

"Every small region would like something unique in its vicinity, something rarely seen," explains Moroń, who grew up 200 meters from the desert.

Moroń, an auburn-haired young woman wearing a striped bronze tee, carries a cordless phone as she offers a tour of the Klucze district office's Desert Information Center, where one day tourists might visit to learn about the local environment.

For now, the center looks like an example of an office in an IKEA showroom, with blank whiteboards and artfully arranged candles crowned with virgin wicks. On the conference table rest cups of cornflower- and gold-tinted sand, while a wall-sized photo shows lumpy cumulus clouds rolling over a pine-ringed field of sand. Inside glass cases are stones and fossils unearthed in the desert, and the district secretary offers refreshments in Pustynia Błędowska–branded teacups emblazoned with project logos.

Klucze didn't want the desert to disappear. Neither did the PSA. But without the deforestation and overuse of the land that kept the natural progression of plant life in check, how were they to reclaim their desert?

The first attempt involved goats. In 2010, Silesia district authorities hired 100 goats for the job of expanding and enhancing the desert. The project's initial managers found goats terrifically successful at chomping down the scrub and grasses that bloomed across the desert floor.

Too soon they also discovered that although the animals proved adept at

destroying leaves and stalks, they were less skilled at consuming root systems. An area of goat-cleared land, briefly and beautifully a desert once more, sprouted fresh shrubs and saplings as soon as the goats relocated to fresh pasture.

Verdict: disaster.

After the regrowth of shrubs and trees following the goat experiment, Klucze authorities assumed control of the project by taking an extraordinary step. They applied for and received environmental conservation funding under the Natura 2000 initiative, a European Union–wide directive to preserve and maintain fragile ecosystems. Other Natura 2000 projects represent more typical conservation efforts, such as preserving a threatened fish population in the Danube River Basin. Of the more than 26,000 funded sites as of 2011, the Polish desert may prove the only conservation of an area created through deforestation and maintained by eradicating native plant life.

Officially titled "Active conservation of priority sand habitats," the €2.6 million ($3.4 million) in funding for the Błędow supports the extension of the desert to its boundaries in 1958, and accomplishes this by uprooting willows, pines, and birch trees — some of which grow here naturally, and some of which are non-native species planted to stop the sand drift.

As a first step, project managers contracted with sappers to scour 400 hectares to a depth of 1.5 meters for any military cast-offs. The project's approved goals include expanding and stabilizing the desert dunes and grasslands, establishing nature trails, producing a guidebook, and welcoming at least 1,000 visitors each year to the newly constructed Desert Information Center.

Which, of course, raises the question, What are 1,000 visitors to do in a tiny fake desert in Poland?

Burning Man and beyond

In addition to establishing the Desert Information Center, the project's managers encourage local artisans to capitalize on the commercial opportunity by developing desert-related souvenirs and handicrafts in advance of the crowds they expect to arrive here. So far, you can buy a stained-glass camel ornament, wooden squares painted with big-lashed cartoon camels, a cheese-filled "Sahara bun," and a local moonshine called "Magic of the Desert."

Children from neighboring towns who are studying Africa in school come to the Błędow on school trips to see their native desert, Pajdak says. University students and researchers from Krakow also visit to conduct studies; some have published papers on the desert's ecosystem. The town of Olkusz, about a 15-minute drive from Chechło, boasts a museum of Saharan African culture and handicrafts, created at the bequest of a Polish couple who lived in Africa for 11 years. The museum has organized events and visits to the desert in conjunction with the PSA.

In the northern section of the desert, the land is flat, and on the horizon looms the Katowice Steelworks. The day I visit, the Błędow is cold and gray, with fog hanging low over neat village houses and dark lilacs swooning from overgrown bushes along the lane leading into the desert. Pajdak says that the name, Błędow, comes from the Polish word for "wandering," referencing the perennial mists that make it easy for visitors to get lost here.

We arrive at a portion of the desert reserved for paratrooper use. Skirting a "Military Area: No Trespassing" sign, we find that another group had preceded ours. Two women, one with a camera and one with a reflector, appear at the cusp of a dune near the shattered bunker painted with African motifs, and below them on the fog-damp sand stands a young man, pale, naked, and, having seen us, making an attempt at modesty with his hands. Someone throws him a towel.

Pajdak speaks Polish to explain the situation, and though the translator deciphers his comment, the tilt of Pajdak's head and the lift of his brows communicate the message without the delay of interpretation.

"Art students," the translator confirms. A military truck barrels onto the scene and tells us all to get lost; they're marking out a perimeter for a paratrooper drop later in the day.

On the ride back to Krakow, Pajdak tells me about a television show he caught on the Polish documentary channel, about an American man who was angry with his girlfriend, so he went to the desert and threw a party, but then the party became a big deal, an annual event that everyone wanted to attend.

Of course I've heard of it, he insists. It takes a moment to place what he's describing.

"Burning Man?" I shout from the back seat, above the rumble of Pajdak's Fiat Uno Fire.

"Tak, tak," he says, yes, yes, that's it.

They'll do something like that, he tells me, and make their summer festival bigger and better, a Little Burning Man, a Burning Man Junior, here in the cold desert of Poland, with the flames of Katowice flickering in the distance.

---

1 Kantor-Mirski, the father of Poland's renowned avant-garde artist Tadeusz Kantor, adopted the pseudonym of Mirski, abandoned his family, and was caught distributing underground newspapers during World War II, after which he was arrested and killed at Auschwitz. His regional history monographs, including the one describing the Błędow, became collector's items.

Down from the Mountaintop

Derham Giuliani charmed nature of its secrets on high.

By TIM HEFFERNAN

Appeared in
Issue 25,
Sept.12, 2013

Years ago I met a man who told me a secret that has stayed evergreen. Derham Giuliani was a self-taught naturalist, the foremost expert on the insects and amphibians of the dry lands in the rain shadow of the Sierra Nevada.

Across four decades, in a labor of patient, painstaking love, he uncovered the hidden lives of the tiny, fragile, and remarkable creatures that live in this vast, harsh, and unremarked-upon corner of the country. Over and over, he made fresh discoveries. The secret he told me was one. What he described is a wonder of the natural world, and as far as I know it remains safe to this day.

Derham lived in what the IRS would classify as poverty, but by all accounts he wanted for little. He lived alone, and was happy that way. He observed, he learned, and he taught. It was a life, and a way of life, to be honored. When I met him I was in my second year of college, at a strange school in a brown valley in the high California desert near the Nevada border. He could have taught me whatever I wanted to know about that desert, but I was young and hasty, and thought the secret was the only valuable thing.

It was not. His life and studies were the gifts. I received them, without being fully aware of their value, "when I was eighteen and nineteen, when it counted," as Edward Hoagland put it.

MPW

No fancy hiking boots; just low-top sneakers. Never jeans; just thrift-store slacks. "He looked sort of like an erudite bum," James Wilson, a friend, says with a laugh.

Sui generis

Derham Giuliani grew up in the Bay Area, fell head over heels for Mother Nature, and resolved never to leave her. As a young man he earned a small living gathering specimens for University of California biologists. He worked in the San Francisco fog and on the misty Farallon Islands.

Then, at some point, he traveled east, away from the ocean and across the mountains to the desert that lies between the Golden State and the forest-green Rockies, where his heart settled. He moved to the little town of Big Pine, named for an incongruous sequoia planted in 1913 to celebrate the opening of a new road and itself named for Teddy Roosevelt.

PTL

He befriended Enid Larsen, a local teacher and naturalist, who invited him to park his truck on her property and live in a spare cabin she owned. Then he began to explore.

Up the well-watered canyons of the Sierra Nevada. Deep into the chalk-dry Nevada desert. Across sand dunes and through pine forests. Day and night, summer and winter, for days and weeks at a time, especially in his beloved White-Inyo Range, the lush Sierras' arid twin — just a few miles from their snowy peaks, but drier, higher, emptier, and to those who fall under their spell, more beautiful.

Type http://magcode.me/ plus a blue code in the margin to visit the related Web page.

Derham would drive his old truck as close as he could to where he wanted to be — which was rarely very close, since he generally wanted to be where people and roads didn't go — and then hike in. No fancy hiking boots; just low-top sneakers. Never jeans; just thrift-store slacks. "He looked sort of like an erudite bum," James Wilson, a friend, says with a laugh. "He also had perhaps the most beautiful stride I've ever seen. The guy could walk."

Atop any notable mountain in the American West you will find a container, left there by an early summiter, with a notebook and a pencil inside: a peak register. When you reach the top, you sign your name. Many registers date back decades and form a sort of community-in-time. Derham's name shows up in them again and again, often in hard-to-reach places where even old registers still have a lot of blank pages.

Denise Waterbury befriended Derham at the White Mountain Research Station, a University of California field institute and the heart of the local scientific community. She recalls climbing Troy Peak, a desolate slab in the empty heart of Nevada. The peak is notable only for the bristlecone pines — the world's longest-lived tree — that speckle its bare slopes. (There are much easier places to see them, including, easiest of all, in the White Mountains themselves, at the end of a paved Forest Service road.)

At the end of the 7,000-foot climb to Troy Peak, Waterbury says, "I thought, 'OK, I don't have to come up here again.' I remember actually saying that to my friends — and then sitting down and opening the register and seeing Derham's name in there six times!"

His name lives on elsewhere, too. At least five species bear it: four insects and a spider, all tiny creatures living in difficult places. There is *Microedus giulianii* (a beetle), *Tescalsia giulianiata* (an alpine moth), and *Xenochelifer derhami* (the spider). There's also Giuliani's dune scarab beetle (*Pseudocotalpa giulianii*), and the tongue-pleasing Giuliani's dubiraphian riffle beetle (*Dubiraphia giulianii*).

Taxonomy rules forbid naming a species for oneself. But a discoverer can name one in honor of another person. And so those tiny *giulianii*s and *derhami*s are a measure of the great respect and affection felt for Derham by the many scientists whose work he supported with his collecting. (These scientists in turn supported him with the small research grants he lived on. Friends and neighbors helped, too: a new pair of binoculars, a repair job; practical needs.)

The names also speak to his wondrous powers of observation, and to the hours he devoted to learning all that was already known of the insects and amphibians in the places he explored. Only that combination of a nature-lover's keen eyes and an expert's mastery of detail allowed him to realize, on a wind-swept flat two and a half miles above sea level in the Whites, that the tiny moth in his net was new to science. He was as unique as his discovery and, like it, born to reach rare heights.

The examined life

"I've never met another naturalist so observant, so knowledgeable, and so will-ing to share his knowledge with you," says Waterbury. And even those who didn't know him have remarked on Derham's generosity with his prodigious learning. Chris Norment, a young biologist at SUNY-Brockport, never met Der-ham but offers gratitude for his work in an online diary:

> I park my car and walk up another arid alluvial fan in the Inyo Mountains, climb for sixteen hundred feet through creosote bush scrub, over desert pavement, and up a boulder-strewn wash. Ninety minutes of dry and sweaty walking brings me into a narrow limestone slot; the sound of falling water drifts down canyon, past a cluster of seep willow.
>
> This looks like slender salamander habitat, and I only have to flip two rocks before I find one — a large, chocolate-brown individual, with a beautiful constella-tion of silver-gray iridophores on its dorsal surface....
>
> This is a good spot, the best I've found so far — and the only reason I know of it is because a biologist showed me an unpublished report by Derham Giuliani (1931–2010), an "old-time" naturalist who spent many years exploring the Inyo, White, and Sierra Nevada mountains.

Friends also note another side of Derham's nature. John Smiley, the former director of White Mountain Research Station, knew him for almost 30 years. "Everybody recognized this quality. I don't know what you'd call it, but I think James Wilson said it best: 'He was just a saintly person.'"

Wilson himself explains: "I can tell you that he's one of the most beloved humans, by the few people who knew him, that I've ever known. Because of the purity of his love of the natural world and the simplicity of his life, he's a para-digm many would aspire to but few of us in this ragingly materialistic culture manage to achieve. He lived in a shack, and he had a truck because he had to [in order] to do his field research. And he loved books." Wilson adds, "He's perhaps the simplest-living person I've ever known."

You can see flashes of Derham's spirit, as a scientist seeking knowledge and a man seeking meaning, in a videotaped interview. With his bright, kindly eyes, white beard, and silver hair, he certainly looks like a schoolbook saint. But it is his carriage and demeanor that mark him as different. He is quiet and still before the camera, where others would giggle and fidget.

PTW

"I've never met another naturalist so observant, so knowledgeable, and so willing to share his knowledge with you." — WATERBURY

And he does something that any writer will recognize as rare: he answers the question he is asked, and when he is done answering, he stops talking. Most of us are hopelessly confessional under even friendly interrogation. We go on and on; we spill our guts as though reticence were a crime. Derham doesn't. His peacefulness is utterly disarming and, well, yes — kind of holy. Although my response is colored by knowing, as I do now, that he likely had already been diagnosed with terminal cancer at the time the video was made.

Derham worked on his archives and continued to take joy in nature right up to his death in September 2010. He seems to have prepared long in advance, and with good humor, for the moment. Commenting in November 2007 on a fatuous article about "green burials," he suggested instead that readers "mimic nature; millions of years of life have prepared the perfect recycling method. With a bit of planning, the vultures, ravens, coyotes, worms, insects, etcetera can be coaxed into doing the job correctly in quite short order."

SJD

Not a rabble rouser

I met this man on two occasions, 15 and 16 summers ago. In no meaningful sense did I know him. Why Derham struck the young me so powerfully is no great mystery, nor is it, if I am honest, entirely complimentary to my character.

James Wilson's "erudite bum" was his friend; to me he was partway a curiosity, an exotic creature that I might poke at for a response. And I was still just young enough to feel free to do so, with the sort of rude, prying questions that are a specialty of precocious children. Wouldn't a pair of real hiking boots be better than those old sneakers? Is it true he often slept in his truck?

But I was also sincerely impressed by Derham, and envious of him. I was falling in love with the wild parts of that country. I took long hikes into it, without maps, to see what I could find. Spend time alone in the desert mountains and pay attention and you inevitably find things: arrowheads, fossils, petroglyphs.

Derham found a gathering of butterflies, in a place where they weren't known to exist in numbers and where they shouldn't have been able to survive for long.

I once found a Joshua tree where it shouldn't have been — too high up, and miles from its nearest kin. Another time I found a pair of structures, like dry-stone weirs, that had been built across the mouths of two small draws. They were not marked on the archaeological surveys I later checked, and I could not guess their purpose, but I could tell that they were ancient: sediment had piled up behind them until it reached their tops.

Every discovery was a hot thrill. The solitude was as continuously refreshing as running water. To spend my life walking alone, seeing things few eyes had seen — to spend my life as Derham spent his — seemed to promise a lifetime of that refreshment and those thrills. I wanted to learn from him how to do it. Writing has not proved a perfect substitute, but it's kept me mostly satisfied.

Why Derham strikes me so powerfully today is not as straightforward. Beyond his kindness, his generosity, and his self-possession, I mean — beyond that life, and way of life, to be honored. But viewed from the different path I chose for my life's work, a lesson from his labors stands out. For all his love of solitude, he worked according to the scientist's code that the value of any discovery lies in sharing it with others. "It's always been traditional among scientists all over the world to be in communication with one another," he says in that video. "To me, this is part of civilization at its best."

Not just the value but the very meaning of discovery has to include that idea of sharing. My reporting isn't really reporting unless it is read. Science doesn't count until the methods and results can be repeated.

Humans have walked the canyon in which those salamanders dwell for thousands of years; Derham was not the first to see the little creatures there. But he was the first to record their presence. Because of that, others can now find them and learn from them, try to keep them safe, miss them if they ever disappear, and try to bring them back if they do.

The secret Derham told me is a rare exception to his openness with his discoveries. It seems he told me and, at most, a few others — and none that I spoke to or could find. I never traveled to vet its truth, but Derham having said it, I believe it without qualms.

Derham found a gathering of butterflies, in a place where they weren't known to exist in numbers and where they shouldn't have been able to survive for long. Were he to have told the world — or were I to — a wonder of nature might have been illuminated. It also might have been overrun by the curious and destroyed.

If it survives, I think it's safest remaining secret. And Derham seemed to think so, too. I take his silence as a final lesson. We spill our guts as if reticence were a crime. But there are times when the crime is to talk.

THE STRAIGHTEST PATH HAS PITFALLS IN LIFE AND HIKING.

By CHRISTA MRGAN

LAUDE

CUM

SUMMIT

Rime ice has encrusted my sneakers when I reach for them at 4:30 a.m. I had forgotten to tuck them under my sleeping bag the night before. I pull them on anyway, cursing softly in the darkness. Roughly 50 yards from the Star Pad (the exposed rock where I sleep most nights this final summer in Yosemite) stands the stone kitchen, warmed just enough by the pilot lights of its old propane stoves.

Being alone there with the battery-powered radio picking up San Francisco's KQED before anyone else in camp has woken is nearly enough to make up for the cold, dark, terrible earliness.

Living and working in Yosemite National Park at the age I did feels a lot like college anyway — without the courses.

Yosemite University

HGH

At the base of an 11,400-foot peak and eight miles from the nearest road, I make breakfast for the 50 or so guests of Vogelsang High Sierra Camp, plus the eight employees who are around that day, then pack myself a bag lunch. It's my fifth summer in Yosemite National Park. I'd lived there for a full year when I first left Florida to take some time off school, and I'd returned every summer until I finished college.

To other misguided youths, I cannot recommend this course of action enough. It allowed me the time and space for the important work of one's early twenties — namely, having adventures of self-discovery — without racking up excess student loan debt, as I no doubt would have had I instead stayed in school, stumbling from one major to another.

Living and working in Yosemite National Park at the age I did feels a lot like college anyway — without the courses. The majority of employees are young, everyone has a roommate, and a communal bathroom serves you and your co-workers. Of course, it's much cheaper than dorm life, and it can be conducive to saving money if your idea of fun is to hike and backpack or rock-climb.

Though I'd had a job of some kind or another since I was 16, the Yosemite lifestyle helped me really learn about the value of money, while still being fairly "safe." It's like training wheels for adulthood in a way that going off to college should be but often isn't.

When you're an employee of DNC (formally, the Delaware North Parks and Resorts at Yosemite, an NPS-authorized concessioner), rent is deducted from your paycheck, and you have the option of being "on meals," another way that working there mimics campus life.

Unlike in college, you can't blow off "class" — in this case, work — whenever you feel like it; but as long as you show up and do your job, you're guaranteed a roof over your head. It also underscores the need to have some kind of marketable skill set, as you get a taste of life as an unskilled laborer.

It tastes like leftover enchiladas.

School of hard knocks

Before my year in Yosemite, I'd found myself studying humanities at the University of South Florida in Tampa, not far from where I was raised. My parents' incomes nudged us into the middle class, but they'd neither planned nor saved

The author sits across from her visiting boyfriend and future husband, Neven Mrgan.

for their children's college educations. Yet it was expected that we would some-how go to college. Never mind the high cost of tuition and the subsequent bur-den of student loans, or how an education might (or in many more cases, might not) later facilitate a career.

"Just go to school or be doomed to failure." That more than a few of my friends — who majored in things like women's studies and English — now work as baristas, servers, and secretaries can attest to this being a mantra in mid-dle-class American households. Not much can be done with an undergraduate degree in humanities, aside from attending grad school or making an incredibly expensive paper airplane.

The time in the park gave me the perspective I needed to decide what I really wanted to study when I returned to school with California residency, in-state tuition, and Pell Grants. It was in Yosemite, either on a mountaintop or in a kitchen, that I decided my work had to be creative and engaging, and involve making something that could have a lasting impact on others as well as be fulfill-

Vogelsang High Sierra Camp. **Photo by Neven Mrgan**

ing in its own right. When I returned to school, I majored in film production and minored in graphic design.

"But that's not practical at all!" I can still hear my mother wail. She preferred the humanities route, picturing me as a tweed-clad college professor. But I loved film and saw it as an industry that would continue to thrive. I figured I'd get some technical chops while doing creative work in school. It was a blast; I even ran my school's film festival one year.

Appeared in
Issue 16,
May 9, 2013

My parents' incomes nudged us into the middle class, but they'd neither planned nor saved for their children's college educations.

Remember that you're standing on a planet that's evolving

Breakfast comprises a kind of frittata and blueberry "scones" — nothing I baked ever turned out quite right at that altitude — eaten with the crew after the last of the guests has finished eating and has filed out of the metal-framed, canvas-covered dining tent. In the High Sierra Camps, where everything arrives and leaves via pack-mule train, organic waste must be kept separate from dry trash and recyclables, so I dutifully scrape my leftovers into the ORG bucket, but leave the camp helpers to clean the kitchen. Another consolation of being the cook and getting up far too early is that other people are on clean-up duty.

My friend/roommate/boss Ellie is drinking matcha and going through paperwork in the corner of the dining tent that serves as the camp check-in and our meager general store.

I tell her, "I'm gonna bag Amelia Earhart Peak; I'll be back around 2:30 to start dinner. It's enchilada night!"

"Leftover enchilada fiesta!" she says, raising her mug.

Vogelsang sits well above the tree line, and the walk to the base of Amelia Earhart is an easy stroll of a couple of miles along the faint, neglected trail to Ireland Lake. Very few among the millions of people who visit Yosemite even make it out of the valley, let alone this far into the backcountry. That day, no one else was in sight. I love solo hikes, but a friend had recently taken a bad fall, which made us all a bit more cautious, and careful to let others know our plans before setting out.

My friend Colin, due to join us at Vogelsang that summer, had fallen nearly 200 feet off the face of Mount Hoffman just a month before. He'd been on a day hike much like this one. Thanks to the quick response of his hiking companions as well as that of the long-time manager of May Lake (a wilderness first responder), he survived. He'd been in a coma for three weeks, and we'd just received word he was showing signs of waking.

I find the summit register, a little metal box tucked into a space between rocks, and pull out the pen and log book within.

As Sierra peaks go, the north side of Amelia Earhart has a fairly gradual slope, but there's a place about three-quarters of the way up where massive slabs of granite overlap steeply, like thick slices of bread arranged in a basket. There are sheer drop-offs on either side. Avoiding the glacier-polished areas I know to be slick, I make my way along and over the slabs one at a time. Leveraging myself up a pile of scattered boulders, I step on a large rock and feel it lurch beneath me. I lose my footing and fall backward onto my butt, sliding a few feet. I catch myself and breathe hard. Pebbles skitter over the edge of the slab and disappear.

It's not a big fall, really; just a slip. It wouldn't even have registered on my personal list of close calls — which includes a broken wrist and nearly falling off the top of a waterfall — but I am briefly struck by the full knowledge of my mortality. Had I gone the way of the pebbles, my friends would've at least known where to look for me, but if I'd sustained life-threatening injuries, no one would've made it in time. So I sit, waiting for the waves of adrenaline to pass, and sing "The Galaxy Song" by Eric Idle (my closest approximation to prayer).

Star trek

I scramble up the rest of the peak without incident. Like many of its Sierra siblings, Amelia Earhart's top portion resembles the rock collection of a particularly careless giant, massive boulders piled up haphazardly. I find the summit register, a little metal box tucked into a space between rocks, and pull out the pen and log book within. It is filled with names, quotes, descriptions of sunsets. I don't remember exactly what I wrote, just that it was about brevity and included a shout-out to Colin.

I stay up there for a while, eating my sandwich and taking in the panorama that will be "my summer backyard" for the very last summer, knowing the season will pass all too quickly. Later, the enchiladas are well received. We make our nightly announcements about bear-safe food and toiletry storage and not burning found wood, and we eat after the guests have left the now-chilly dining tent.

I say my goodnights and wash up, then slide into my sleeping bag on the Star Pad, remembering to tuck my sneakers beneath it. I stare up at the Milky Way and feel intensely sad to know I'll eventually leave that place; it has never left me. I'd do it all again, and I hope my daughter, Olive, does it too. Unless she gets into Harvard.

Laid Out

A hen's egg-producing years are short; her life is relatively long.

By NANCY GOHRING

I t wasn't until a day or two after I moved into my first house in Seattle in 2001 that I noticed that my neighbor had chickens. Cool! I thought. Back then, keeping urban chickens was unusual, although Seattle was progressive among US cities for allowing it.

But living next door to chickens didn't turn out as great as I'd hoped. My neighbor took free range so literally that the chickens freely roamed the whole yard all day every day. With big gaps under the fence, it was inevitable that they'd make their way into my yard.

I was enraged as I watched them peck tiny peppers off plants that I had painstakingly nursed to life despite the city's chilly, gray climate. I was mortified to learn that hosing chicken poo off my patio just before guests arrive for a barbecue is the absolute worst way to get rid of it. (Wet chicken poo reeks.) And I felt like a fool chasing someone else's chickens around my yard, especially since I wasn't sure what I'd do if I caught one.

Fortunately, she moved away a couple of years later, ending our arguments about her chickens.

Since then, keeping chickens has become popular in urban areas nation-

Appeared in
Issue 25,
Sept. 12, 2013

LKJ

wide. In many cities, chicken owners get together at barter events or online to swap tips and tackle issues facing people who are revitalizing this practice — like keeping neighbors happy.

The latest topic consuming this community is how best to manage the end of life. Any creature ages and eventually dies, so it was only a matter of time before complications arose for chicken custodians. Traditionally, older chickens, past their egg-laying days, went into the soup pot.

But since many contemporary chicken keepers didn't grow up on farms, they don't know how to off a bird. Decapitating a chicken is beyond the repertoire and outside the sensibility (and available equipment) of most urban dwellers, who aren't used to killing animals much bigger than a spider.

But whether functional farm animal or beloved pet or even member of the family, more people are having end-of-life planning discussions. Many are starting to face their chickens' ultimate retirement.

Chicken or the egg

Hens lay lots of eggs for only a couple of years. After that, egg production quickly declines. Since the birds can live for 10 years or more, owners are faced with a conundrum: pay to feed and care for chickens for eight years or longer with no egg return, or somehow get rid of them humanely by killing them or giving them to someone who will care for them.

Many people are completely unaware of this. They blithely buy a couple of chicks because they're cute and it's the popular thing to do, without being prepared for what comes down the line.

XMQ

CRT

Unwilling to kill their chickens or continue to pay for their feed, these people try to give them away. A recent NBC News article quotes the owner of Chicken Run Rescue, a Minneapolis organization that takes in unwanted chickens, who says that the number of birds brought to the rescue has grown from 50 in 2001 to 500 last year.

Laurel Menoche and her husband, John Fox, took the responsible route to chicken ownership. They spent a couple of years deciding to get chickens, vigorously debating what to do when the hens stopped laying. Today, Menoche has six hens at her Seattle home. The first time she saw a chicken killed, it was pretty grim. "It was shocking for me," she says. "The reality was I got upset. I was crying and forcing myself to watch."

Type http://magcode.me/ plus a blue code in the margin to visit the related Web page.

In Seattle, an unscientific measure of how many people are unprepared to deal with older hens is the regularity with which people post to the Seattle Farm Co-op newsgroup in search of a home for a hen that's no longer laying eggs. The Co-op was formed to bulk buy organic chicken feed, and its active newsgroup hosts discussions on everything from raising pygmy goats in the city to how best to keep raccoons at bay.

Charmaine Slaven, one of the founders of the Seattle Farm Co-op, has been on a mission not only to educate potential chicken owners that they need to think about the full life span of their cute, fuzzy chicks but also to teach people

Decapitating a chicken is beyond the repertoire and outside the sensibility (and available equipment) of most urban dwellers.

how to dispatch chickens humanely. She grew up in Montana eating animals her family raised. "I was one of the people who got to learn these skills from my parents," she says.

Slaven believes that all chicken-raising classes should devote a portion of the class to the end-of-life issue. In fact, the Co-op sells chicks only once a year and requires buyers to first take a chick-care class in which attendees typically discuss what happens when laying ends. The classes prompt people "to think ahead and have a plan for their flock, whether they are of the chickens-as-pets school or the chickens-as-food-animals school," she says. The classes "ensure there's not as much impulse buying."

Compounding the issue is that chicken owners often start regarding their brood as pets. Some birds are quite beautiful. When I visited Menoche, her birds came running at the sight of her, perhaps hopeful she'd have a special treat to offer.

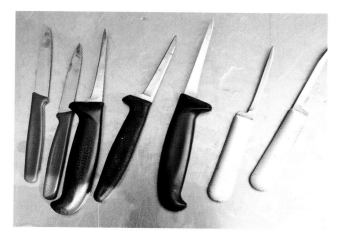

Ruling the roost

After Menoche realized that she might grow attached to the birds, she and her husband spent a long time discussing how they would manage the chickens' life spans. He wanted to cull and replace hens that stopped laying. She wasn't sure how she'd feel about killing them.

"I had a hard time agreeing to something that had an unknown emotion element. What if I loved each and every one?" Menoche wrote during one of many discussions of this topic on the Co-op newsgroup.

Eventually, they agreed to keep one or maybe two older hens as pets. Complicating that decision was that at the time, the max number of chickens allowed by law was five, so if two weren't laying, they'd have only three egg-producing hens. (The City of Seattle has now upped the number to eight but has also banned roosters.)

From early on, Menoche was adamant that she learn to dispatch chickens herself. "If you keep having chickens, you'll probably run out of friends willing to do it for you," she says.

Not only that, you might be faced with a situation where you need to end a hen's life without delay. Urban chickens have plenty of predators, including dogs and raccoons. "If you come across your chicken and it needs to be put down now, you don't have time for the vet or to look it up on YouTube and botch it and feel guilty for the rest of your life," she says.

Within a year of getting chickens, Menoche and Fox went to a chicken slaughter class put on by the Seattle Farm Co-op, the one that left Menoche in tears. Less emotional about it, Fox ended up slaughtering a chicken in the class; Menoche didn't.

A year later, Menoche realized she needed to attend another class. She hadn't yet had the need to put down a chicken. She wanted more confidence, and she wanted to make sure it was something she could actually do. "I think a lot of women assume their male partners will deal with it," she says.

GXD

Fox offered to attend the second class. "I said, 'No, I'll just hide behind you,'" she says. "So I did it without him and actually dispatched a chicken. It was a big step for me."

Despite all her thoughtfulness around keeping chickens, Menoche, surely like others in her shoes, hasn't always followed the plan. "I did what I said I never would do and [brought] a chicken to the vet," she says. "But she was special."

Their favorite, the one they'd decided they'd keep past her prime laying years, developed a condition that prevented her from digesting many foods. The vet sent them home with antibiotics and suggested they not have high hopes. If the antibiotics didn't help, there wouldn't be much that could be done.[1]

Two weeks later Menoche came home from work and the hen "was in a horrible state." This, though, was just the scenario she'd planned for when she took the chicken slaughtering class twice; her husband was out of town. "I knew what to do, and I instantly left her alone and went in the house and started getting prepared," she says.

From early on, Menoche was adamant that she learn to dispatch chickens herself. "If you keep having chickens, you'll probably run out of friends willing to do it for you," she says.

Just a few things have changed in the art of chicken slaughtering. These days, the pros recommend that instead of using a hatchet, with which you might cut off a finger accidentally, you use a very sharp knife to slice the bird's jugular.[2]

Menoche thinks that one other aspect may have changed too. "I might say that we've learned a lot over the years about animal suffering," she says. "What we teach in the Co-op class is to hold and support them in a way that keeps them calm. We use a very sharp knife. If you can recall ever being cut with a really sharp knife, it takes some time to actually feel pain.

"My hope is that the chickens are close, if not already in death before there is much discomfort. If you only have a few chickens, you can take the time to do it with empathy and respect."

Fowl way to die

There are other options besides killing your chickens when they stop laying eggs. For instance, some farms, and organizations like Minneapolis's Chicken Run Rescue, will take older hens. But it turns out that retiring to a rescue ranch may not be a great life for the chickens that the urban farmer cares so much about.

"Anybody who has integrated chickens [into a flock] knows it ain't pretty," says Menoche. It's even worse moving a chicken from a back yard where it lives with a handful of other birds to a farm, where the chicken will likely have to forage for food, competing with many more birds. "It's like taking a Chihuahua and bringing it into an established pack of pit bulls," she says.

TSW

WXV

Erica Strauss, who runs the popular blog Northwest Edible Life, offers another reason people shouldn't consider such farms, in a post where she argues passionately about why all chicken owners should know how to cull their own birds. "You do not get to embrace the idea of a more intimate relationship with your food chain and then make that food chain — the food chain you specifically set up — someone else's problem when shit gets real," she writes.

Giving the hens away to anybody, whether to keep or kill, shouldn't be an option, she says. "There is a local urban farming message board that is filled — filled — with people trying to give away their three-year-old chicken to a 'good home.' Are you kidding me? You own the chicken. Your home is a good home. And once it's not, your soup pot is a good soup pot," she writes.

Instead of killing a bird after it's not producing many eggs, owners can keep them as pets, paying to feed and care for them. That expense might be fine for people who want to keep the bird just like any other pet that doesn't return much but a bit of beauty and love. But in fact it might not be more humane than killing it.

"Most of our laying hens don't die peacefully from 'old age,'" Slaven writes in a discussion on the newsgroup. These days, they are bred for egg production and are more likely to develop "various cancers and other wasting diseases before crossing the rainbow bridge," she writes. "This is why I think culling the flock is more humane. Chickens can live for a very long time in an unhealthy, suffering state."

Crossing the road

Slaven has taken it upon herself to teach people how to dispatch their chickens, often by teaching classes through the Co-op. At first, she tried to convince another large popular gardening organization in town, Seattle Tilth, to add classes about chicken slaughter. After all, that group offers a number of other classes designed to help urban dwellers start keeping chickens.

But so far, Tilth hasn't added slaughtering to its class roster. "It came down to them [being] scared of liability and people losing interest in chickens," Slaven says.

Tilth hasn't had much demand for slaughter classes, says Liza Burke, communications director at Seattle Tilth. If people ask about slaughtering their chickens, the organization refers people to the Co-op as well as to Farmstead Meatsmith, a butcher in the Puget Sound region that also offers classes.

Slaven says it's true that Tilth sends people to the Co-op. But some of those referrals show how unprepared some chicken owners are for dispatching their birds. Tilth is "often sending troubled chicken owners to us after they are in a pinch with their old hens, not realizing that this was going to be a part of their chicken ownership path," Slaven wrote recently on the newsgroup, in response to a discussion about Strauss's blog post.

For her part, Menoche said she and her husband feel good about spending the amount of time they did considering how to handle the end of life for her chickens before they got them. "My husband probably had this fear that we'd end up with this big petting zoo, with 20 chickens and none of them laying," she says. Instead, they're happy with their flock of six.

They also know that beyond simply and literally putting the hens out to pasture, when the time comes, they're prepared to help their chickens cross the final road to get to the other side.

1 Susan Orlean, the author of *The Orchid Thief* and an animal lover, wrote in 2009 about the revived trend of owning chickens, and the loss of one of her beloved brooders.

2 That link takes you to a *Seattle* magazine article written by regular *Magazine* contributor Joe Ray, who also provided the photos for this article – which were taken when he attended the class he discusses in that story.

A Bicycle Built for Six

The Netherlands has elevated bikes far above cars in the transportation hierarchy.

By LIANNE BERGERON

The Netherlands is home to over 18 million bicycles. This is a staggering number when you consider that the population is only 16.5 million people. About 84 percent of the Dutch own a bike, which works out to about 1.3 bikes per active cyclist. The country has close to 35,000 km (22,000 miles) of cycling infrastructure, which in a country the size of a peanut — or more precisely, the size of Maryland — is quite a lot.

I am a Canadian girl who used to drive everywhere, had her license when she was 16 and a day, and managed to put more mileage on her parents' car before she turned 20 than in the following 20 years. Now I live just outside of Amsterdam and own four of those 18 million bicycles.

The author cycles her kids around in a cargo bike. **Photos by Lianne Bergeron**

I have a bike for the city, which I leave parked by the bus stop so that I can get around Amsterdam. I have a regular bike here at home that I use for quick zips around town. There's a cargo bike (or *bakfiets*) for family outings. And I still use my old L.L. Bean cycle, purchased over 20 years ago, for the occasional long-distance ride.

I've never tallied up my total kilometers biked over the last 15 years, but a rough calculation has me nearing 30,000 km (18,000 miles). That's like biking across Canada six times — and I've driven it only once.

For every purpose, a bike

My cargo bike is built for six. It seats four children in the front, one on the back, and me. If it's not full of kids, it's full of groceries, school bags, other bikes, beehives — my *husband's* hobby — and the occasional borrowed chair or table for a party. Every day, I get up, have breakfast, and take my kids to school and head to work on this bike — every day, rain or shine, snow or sleet, wind or wind. *There is a lot of wind where I live.*

I was working in Amsterdam when I met my husband, who is Dutch. I've stayed, however, not only because of the marriage or the weather or the drug laws. It's the biking and the lifestyle that comes with it. Before living here, I biked around the block as a tyke, and occasionally to school. Now I have the Dutch mindset: use a bike where you can, when you can. I never think about using the car. Rather, I think about which of my four bikes I need to pull out.

The Dutch government has made it easy by providing the infrastructure needed for safe and efficient cycling. Creating bike paths and lanes is important, but a lot of other components make it into an ecosystem: bike signage, bike traffic lights, bike repair shops, bike-purchase tax breaks, and bike right-of-way, as well as a well-designed bike parking system.

This is further enhanced by the diversity of types of bikes and the accessories designed for them. Some bikes, like my cargo one, carry kids and groceries. There are clip-ons for baby buggies or dog leashes, and crates in the front and bags on the back for extra carrying space. Add some good old-fashioned tie wraps on the tires in the winter, and you're ready for biking in the snow.

There are taxi bikes, foldable-portable bikes the size of a small suitcase for use with public transport, cargo bikes with two or three wheels, kid bikes, speed bikes, back-break bikes...and the list continues. Electric bikes are gaining market

Appeared in
Issue 19,
June 20, 2013

LFR

share by enabling the elderly and others to cycle while using the extra support of the bike generator. There is, quite literally, a bike for every occasion.

This becomes clear in another remarkable number: over a quarter of all trips in this country are made by bike, with up to 59 percent of them within cities. The national daily biking average is 2.6 km (1.6 mi.), and that number includes trips by kids and the elderly. Denmark follows, with a 1.6 km average, and the United States lags at 0.1 km. The percentage of the elderly still using bikes for daily trips is 24 percent, double that of Germans and Danes.

Even though there are all these bikes on the road, there are per capita fewer biking accidents here than in any other country. There is an overall acknowledgment that bikes are just as important as cars.

The happy lifestyle of the Dutch is well known and much envied. Biking is clearly a part of it.

Even the Romans are biking

Cities around the world have started to promote bike-sharing systems, which make it possible to use a bike without having to own it or find a place to stow it. In the largest cities, such storage is unavailable or expensive, and bikes with any value that are left outside are stolen. (Bikes are stolen in Amsterdam, too, and many people have two locks on their bikes; I have two for my city bike. However, I've lost only one bike to thieves here, and that was 20 years ago.)

Some cities have free bikes; others work with companies that charge for use, as with car sharing. These systems place bikes or bike parking near stations or end points in their public transport infrastructure and encourage people to bike as a component of a commute, when taking kids to school, or when running errands.

This innovation began in Amsterdam back in 1965. The city had made free bikes available for anyone to use. Although it wasn't a huge success here, it did lay the groundwork for other cities to embrace and develop their own bike-sharing systems.

YMT

NFS

Paris has the biggest such system in Europe, second worldwide only to Beijing's. It is run by the city and has over 24,000 bikes available for Parisians

Type http://magcode.me/ plus a blue code in the margin to visit the related Web page.

and tourists alike. New York just added its own option — currently going through the teething pains of software problems — with 6,000 bikes and plans to grow to 10,000.

Between sharing and better infrastructure, the city of London's number of cyclists has tripled over the past decade. London has huge ambitions to become a cycling capital, modeling a lot of its vision on the Dutch system. The Danes are already ahead of the game, with newly built bike highways, and even the Romans are joining in, having purchased more bikes this year than cars, a first in over 50 years. It's no longer an experiment; it's a movement well underway.

Great legs!

City planners and policymakers seem at last to be putting serious effort and money behind making biking a routine, safe, and reasonable part of transportation infrastructure. It's a positive situation in every way: less traffic congestion, fewer emissions, and better legs for everyone. (On that last point, just ask my husband.) Biking can also reduce health-care costs and both improve the quality of and lengthen lives.

Because bikes are affordable (or can even be given away), cycling provides a more level playing field for those who can't afford a car or who devote more money than they can afford to using one.

The happy lifestyle of the Dutch is well known and much envied. Biking is clearly a part of it. When I bike, I arrive at my destination already feeling good. I have avoided the stress of sitting in a traffic jam and can park anywhere. Imagine spreading those feelings around an entire population.

Sometimes it's a challenging workout, with wind, hills, rain, or a full load, so I bike a little slower. And sometimes I would rather take the car. But I don't. It's my policy: I do it for me, and I want my kids to understand that, when possible, it's better for everyone if we bike.

Three Strikes, You Shout

Moneyball documented a change in baseball, but not everyone has done their homework.

By PHILIP MICHAELS

♦♦♦
Appeared in
Issue 27,
Oct. 10, 2013

When you wonder why strikeouts are designated as a κ on a baseball scorecard, please direct your complaints to Henry Chadwick, an Englishman by birth and a sportswriter by trade, who adopted the cricket box score around 1859 to create a record of exactly what transpired in a baseball game.

Chadwick gets credit for establishing the use of consistent statistics against which multiple games, teams, and seasons could be compared. But despite that early start, baseball executives, sportswriters, and fans spent most of the next 144 years making decisions from the gut: observation and experience trumped any underlying story that numbers might have told.

But a change took place that moved numeric wonkiness from periodicals like *The Bill James Baseball Abstract* or Web sites like Baseball Prospectus, which were for a long while the sole concern of hardcore enthusiasts, into the broader sphere of public consciousness.

We can circle the date on the calendar when this happened: it was in 2003, when *Moneyball*, by Michael Lewis, hit bookshelves.

TCB

MYV

Illustration by Jenn Manley Lee

Trim figures

Subtitled "The Art of Winning an Unfair Game," *Moneyball* outlined how the Oakland Athletics were able to pursue champagne aspirations on a near-beer budget. For the 2002 season that Lewis chronicles in *Moneyball*, the A's won 103 games, tying the New York Yankees for the best record in baseball. The A's spent a shade under $42 million on player salaries to win those ballgames; the Yankees spent in the neighborhood of $126 million.[1]

The blueprint outlined by Lewis could essentially be boiled down to: stop trusting old assumptions and start looking at hard data. Other teams overpaid players who tallied up empty stats like batting average and runs batted in; the A's looked for undervalued players who excelled at getting on base. (Or, to put it another way, not making outs.)

While their opponents were busy bunting and stealing bases, the A's were drilling into the minds of their players and coaches that those strategies didn't pay off. And when it came time to scout players for the amateur draft, the A's defied the conventional wisdom of the era by favoring collegiate players over high schoolers, preferring the predictability of performance over projecting what an 18-year-old might one day become.

"Too many people make decisions based on outcome rather than process," then–assistant general manager Paul DePodesta tells Lewis at one point in the book. He's talking about a particular at-bat in a particular regular season game, but really, that quote could be stamped on every other page of *Moneyball* and still be contextually appropriate.

I was an A's season ticket holder (right-field bleacher seats) during the season Lewis wrote about in *Moneyball* as well as during the year the book came out. And for me — and I suspect a good many A's fans — the book offered not so much a glimpse into another way of looking at the game we love as it did a validation of our choice in teams.

Being an A's fan means forgoing the certainty of meaningful postseason baseball (something the dilettantes who've pledged their troth to the New York Yankees take for granted) in favor of a greater ideal.[2] To root for Oakland is to root for the beauty of revealing greater truths about baseball, about life over mere championships.

A's fans have to overlook a crumbling stadium and the series of penurious owners since the beloved Walter Haas went to the big ballyard in the sky so that we can live and die with the team we love.[3] And what *Moneyball* told us was that we had chosen wisely. "Your team is doing things correctly," the book might as well have said. "Smart, intelligent fans realize that, even if braying sports talk radio types do not."

If we felt something of a vicarious thrill thanks to *Moneyball*, imagine how the people actually profiled in the book made out. The book became something of a sensation in business settings, where its themes of exploiting market inefficiencies and finding value where your visionless competitors did not resonated.

Billy Beane, the A's general manager, became a popular figure on the corporate speaking circuit, which he remains on a decade later. (In fact, while the A's were fighting for a division title in September, Beane jetted off to Prague to fulfill one of his corporate obligations.) At any rate, you know you've won the acclaim of the larger world when Brad Pitt is tasked with playing you in the movie.[4]

Beane counters

The baseball establishment, however, was not so smitten with the book. And that's understandable. When the central premise of your book is that a lot of people running teams do dumb things for no good reason, the people doing those dumb things may not appreciate the constructive criticism.

The blowback came not just from Beane's fellow GMs and the baseball scouts who felt that *Moneyball* gave short shrift to their role in spotting talent, but also from writers and columnists who had appointed themselves Guardians of the Game. Antipathy from the former was certainly understandable; the reaction of the latter, though, reeked of a kind of anti-intellectual hostility to anything that challenged conventional wisdom.

Lewis wound up detailing the anti-*Moneyball* reaction from within baseball's establishment in a postscript added to a later edition of the book, titled "Inside Baseball's Religious War." "There are many ways to embarrass The Club," Lewis wrote, referring to the coterie of old-school baseball executives and beat writers making lemon faces about his book, "but being bad at your job isn't one of them. The greatest offense a Club member can commit is not ineptitude but disloyalty."

And so the critics took their shots — at the A's, at Beane, at anyone who thought the team might be on to something with how it was approaching the game of baseball. The A's weren't a *real* success story, the critics suggested,

     Type http://magcode.me/ plus a blue code in the margin to visit the related Web page.

because the team hadn't won a World Series using Beane's crazy schemes. (It's easy to see how Oakland might have been able to out-think people who found the results of a five-game sample size more illustrative than a full 162-game season.) Billy Beane was an egomaniac, they griped. (As compared to the selfless, modest souls who otherwise find success in sports, one might counter.) An especially laughable contingent of the Flat Earth Society wing of baseball commentariat even concluded that *Moneyball* wasn't the work of Lewis — who after all had only written *Liar's Poker* and *The New New Thing*, among other books — but rather of Beane himself.

PFQ, BQB

The most strident voice in that chorus belonged to Joe Morgan, who used his position as both a Hall of Fame player and lead baseball analyst for ESPN's *Sunday Night Baseball* to routinely blast everything about Moneyball at the slightest provocation. Morgan's rhetorical assault on the book might have proven more effective had he not only bothered to properly identify the author but actually read the damn thing, too.

"I played The Game," Morgan says in a 2005 *SF Weekly* profile that perfectly illustrates the obstinacy that greeted Moneyball in some quarters. "You're reading it from a book. I played. I watched. I see everything. I know what happens out there…. My baseball knowledge is accumulated over 20 years of playing, 20 years of watching The Game, so that's what I care about. I can't care if next week somebody comes up with a new way to evaluate The Game. Am I supposed to say, 'Aw, that's good. I'll go that way now'?"

PCL

It shouldn't matter, of course, that Joe Morgan has to perform mental and verbal gymnastics to explain how a team that wins 103 games on a workman's wages is, in fact, a miserable failure. It shouldn't bug me that Bruce Jenkins, the baseball beat writer whom I grew up reading but who has now become the sort of "old man yells at cloud" columnist who invites parody and routinely peppers his columns with diatribes about "stats-crazed dunces" who are ruining baseball for all right-thinking people.

NGT, XWX

VQB

But it does — and not just in the tribal "someone is saying something bad about the team I like" way. These are people paid to write and commentate about baseball, and when it came to one of the biggest shifts in how people think about that sport, Morgan and Jenkins and their ilk couldn't be bothered to do the assigned reading.

Well, we've only had a decade since *Moneyball*'s publication, not the 20 years Joe Morgan demands to reach any concrete conclusions. Still, there's been a marked shift in the attitude toward the notions in what Lewis called a book about an idea — though it would be a bit premature to declare total victory for that idea just yet.

This means WAR

Flip through *Moneyball* these days, and the ideas seem fairly quaint and self evident, like someone excitedly telling you something that you thought had long been accepted as common knowledge. These days, I can launch ESPN.com's Gamecast feature for real-time play-by-play accounts and get calculations for how likely it is that a run will score if there's a runner on first and nobody out in an inning. A mainstream site like ESPN offering that kind of math in 2003 would have been unthinkable.

During last year's debate over the American League Most Valuable Player award, an advanced stat like WAR (Wins Above Replacement, a nifty way for calculating a player's value against his peers) got bandied about alongside traditional numbers like RBI and batting average. (True, a lot of columnists brought up WAR just to dismiss it out of hand — "WAR, what is it good for?" was the lowbrow pun of these sorts of columns — but still: baby steps.)

After a five-season fallow period, the A's got back to winning, first with an improbable division crown in 2012 and then with a slightly more expected triumph this season. The team has found a new market inefficiency to exploit: platooning, in which the A's find one player who can mash right-handed pitchers and another who can do the same to left-handers, and pay each far less than what an overvalued everyday player might command.

It's also worth noting that the A's of 2013 do things that the team profiled in the 2003 book never would have considered, like selecting high school players with first-round draft picks. That's because the lessons of *Moneyball* weren't a series of rules carved in stone and handed down by a bearded prophet to his acolytes in Oakland; rather, it was a state of mind about identifying things your competitors were failing to do and jumping on them. "The point is not to have the highest on-base percentage," Lewis tries to explain in his postscript, using small words so that the book's critics might be able to finally grok the moral of the story, "but to win games as cheaply as possible."

It's a lesson other teams quickly caught on to. The Boston Red Sox, owned by a commodities trader named John Henry, were soon embracing a lot of the principles espoused in *Moneyball* and wound up with two World Series titles to show for it. (The $100 million-plus payroll also helped, admittedly.) The Tampa Bay Rays, as sad sack a franchise you could have found in 2003, had their own statistical rethink on how to assemble a winning baseball team; they've just completed their sixth consecutive winning season.[5]

In fact, of the five teams that are contending with Oakland for the American League pennant this fall, four of them are well known in the baseball business for their fascination with number-crunching. (The fifth, the Detroit Tigers, seem content to pursue a strategy in which they spend owner Mike Illitch's Little Caesars money on fat guys who can hit baseballs great distances.) Even the most stats-averse teams have someone tucked into a cubicle somewhere poring over spreadsheets, even if they're not exactly sure what to do with those numbers.

ZGT

Still balking

If analytics have found their way into most corners of baseball, the last holdouts seem to be the people who write and talk about the game for a living. To be sure, analysis-heavy sites like Baseball Prospectus and Fangraphs have their followings, and a number of sportswriters — chief among them is Joe Posnanski — have incorporated talk about advanced stats into their coverage.

CYV

Some of the more vocal opponents of the modern stat-based approach in general and *Moneyball* in particular have lost their platform. Joe Morgan, who thought everything about the book was a joke, became a bit of a joke himself thanks to FireJoeMorgan.com, which made a sport of taking him and other logic-challenged sports pundits to task for their facts-averse commentary.[6] Morgan was also removed from his *Sunday Night Baseball* gig a few seasons back, but before we take to the streets to rejoice, keep in mind that one of his replacements was the sharp-as-a-bowling-ball John Kruk.[7]

DKT

Still, buy a newspaper, fire up a Web site, turn on a cable sports channel, and you're likely to come across someone trotting out the same "nerds in a basement with a calculator" dismissal of baseball analytics or acting as if *Moneyball*, and all the writing that came before and after it, never existed. They're the soldiers marooned on a remote island who haven't heard that the fight is over — except they have access to mass media.

For a particularly dispiriting example, look no further than the MLB Network, a cable channel that has 24 hours of programming to fill and is largely populated by ex-players mouthing the same empty platitudes about How To Play The Game that were statistically disproven years ago. One of the lone nods the network makes toward acknowledging the influence statistical analysis has on the game is an hour-long show called MLB *Now*, but even this is framed as a tedious debate in which a stats-savvy analyst is pitted against an ex-player, and they mostly talk over each other at ear-splitting volume.

"You think that the average fan is wrapped up in WAR and all these asinine, dopey statistical thoughts that you guys can come up with," an MLB *Now* guest named Chris Russo shouted at the stats-minded host on a recent episode that I had to grit my teeth to get through for the purposes of this article. "*Watch the ballgames*," he added in a voice that would have had to have been lowered several decibels to be considered at the top of his lungs. "If you watch the ballgames, you can figure out who is a good player, who is not a good player."

Well, that's an argument, I suppose. Not as convincing as "Because, OK?" but we'll accept it if only to move on.

Say it's so, Joe

"Basically, everything you know about baseball when you are 14 years old, you know from baseball announcers," a fellow named Voros McCracken tells Michael Lewis in *Moneyball*. Fortunately, McCracken — who did some pioneering research that revealed pitchers can control walks, strikeouts, and home runs but very little else about balls hit into play — had his eyes opened by some of the early writing done by baseball statistic trailblazer Bill James. "Here was this guy who was telling me that at least 80 percent of what baseball announcers told me was complete bullshit, and then explained very convincingly why it was."

And that's the good news, 10 years after *Moneyball*'s release. There are a lot more people like Bill James explaining to even more people like Voros McCracken that the stuff they're hearing from baseball pundits shouldn't go unchallenged. "Teenagers [are] discovering the world for the first time," baseball writer Rany Jazayerli said on a recent episode of the Baseball Show, which he co-hosts. "So you have no preconceived notions that you need to get rid of when you read something that has the power of truth of behind it."

The people who read *Moneyball* as teenagers and had enough talent to play baseball are just coming into their own as Major Leaguers.[8] The ones who became sportswriters are working their way up the chain in journalism, where they'll eventually supplant the columnists who see advanced stats as something to be derided instead of understood. And the rest, the vast majority who simply remain fans of the game, will wonder why anyone ever argued about something so obvious.

"The world is run by people of a certain age," Jazayerli said in his podcast. "And once people who grew up with these principles reach a point in their life where they are naturally in positions of influence, that's when you'll start to see changes made."

Just in time for the next revolution.

---

1   It's not like Lewis got lucky by picking an aberration of a season: between 1999 and 2006, the A's enjoyed winning seasons every year. Only the Yankees and the Atlanta Braves won more baseball games.

2   I will not claim to be an A's fan by birth. I grew up in Southern California, which meant rooting for the Dodgers even after my family moved to the Bay Area and whatever live baseball I could attend was usually an A's game. I stuck with the Dodgers right up until News Corp. bought the team, because, really, what sensible person can endure living and dying for something owned by Rupert Murdoch. I switched my allegiance to the A's, and this only becomes awkward during discussions of the 1988 World Series, which ended well for me at the time.

3   Walter Haas was an heir of Levi Strauss & Co. who essentially bought the club to give his son-in-law something to do, and he treated the A's as one of the many civic and cultural institutions he helped bankroll. My favorite Walter Haas story, recounted in Glenn Dickey's *Champions*, is when Haas was touring the Oakland Coliseum shortly after buying the team and noticed a storeroom full of official Major League baseballs. "Do you think I can have one of those?" he asked the stadium staff. They decided that he could.

4   Pitt was nominated for an Academy Award for his portrayal of Billy Beane in the 2011 movie adaptation of *Moneyball*. Your author, who plays an extra in the crowd at the Oakland-Kansas City game near the movie's conclusion, was not nominated for anything.

5   Like the A's, the Rays also have a book chronicling their reversal of fortune, called *The Extra 2%*. I should disclose that the author of the book, Jonah Keri, once worked at the same newspaper I did. That fact doesn't make me inclined to endorse his book; the fact that I have beat him at poker, however, does. NYN

6   Sadly, FireJoeMorgan closed its doors five years ago, because the people working on it got too busy creating TV shows like *Parks & Recreation*. NNQ

7   Kruk once predicted that Randy Johnson would win 30 games a season pitching for the New York Yankees – a bold forecast considering that in an era of five-man rotations even the most durable starters get around 35 starts a year. To be fair to Kruk, Johnson did win 34 games as a Yankee, though it took him two seasons to do that.

8   An example would be Brandon McCarthy, a pitcher who used advanced statistics to reshape his career. YBV

YOU ARE BORING

Everything was going great until you showed up. You see me across the crowded room, make your way over, and start talking at me. And you don't stop.

You are a Democrat, an outspoken atheist, and a foodie. You like to say "Science!" in a weird, self-congratulatory way. You wear jeans during the day, and fancy jeans at night. You listen to music featuring wispy lady vocals and electronic bloop-bloops.

You really like coffee, except for Starbucks, which is the worst. No wait — Coke is the worst! Unless it's Mexican Coke, in which case it's the best.

Pixar. Kitty cats. Uniqlo. Bourbon. Steel-cut oats. Comic books. Obama. Fancy burgers.

You listen to the same five podcasts and read the same seven blogs as all your pals. You stay up late on Twitter making hashtagged jokes about the event that everyone has decided will be the event about which everyone jokes today. You love to send withering @ messages to people like Rush Limbaugh — of course, those notes are not meant for their ostensible recipients, but for your friends, who will chuckle and retweet your savage wit.

TELL ME MORE ABOUT YOUR FOOD BLOG, PLEASE.

By **SCOTT SIMPSON**

143

†††
Appeared in
Issue 4,
Nov. 22, 2012

You are boring. So, so boring.

Don't take it too hard. We're all boring. At best, we're recovering bores. Each day offers a hundred ways for us to bore the crap out of the folks with whom we live, work, and drink. And on the Internet, you're able to bore *thousands of people at once.*[1]

A few years ago, I had a job that involved listening to a ton of podcasts. It's possible that I've heard more podcasts than anyone else — I listened to at least a little bit of tens of thousands of shows. Of course, the vast majority were so bad I'd often wish microphones could be sold only to licensed users. But I did learn how to tell very quickly whether someone was interesting or not.

When people tell stories, they think about how to communicate the entirety of their experience to someone else.

The people who were interesting told good stories. They were also inquisitive: willing to work to expand their social and intellectual range. Most important, interesting people were also the best listeners. They knew when to ask questions. This was the set of people whose shows I would subscribe to, whose writing I would seek out, and whose friendship I would crave. In other words, those people were the opposite of boring.

Here are the three things they taught me.

Listen, then ask a question

I call it Amtrak Smoking Car Syndrome (because I am old, used to smoke, thought that trains were the best way to get around the country, and don't really understand what a syndrome is). I'd be down in the smoking car, listening to two people have a conversation that went like this:

> *Stranger #1: Thing about my life.*
> *Stranger #2: Thing about my life that is somewhat related to what you just said.*
> *Stranger #1: Thing about my life that is somewhat related to what you just said.*
> *Stranger #2: Thing about my life...*

Next stop: Boringsville, Population: 2. There's no better way to be seen as a blowhard than to constantly blow, hard. Instead, give a conversation some air. Really listen. Ask questions; the person you're speaking with will respect your inquisitiveness and become more interested in the exchange. "Asking questions makes people feel valued," said former Virgin America VP Porter Gale, "and they transfer that value over to liking you more."

Watch an old episode of *The Dick Cavett Show*. Cavett is an engaged listener, very much part of the conversation, but he also allows his partner to talk as well. He's not afraid to ask questions that reveal his ignorance, but it's also clear he's no dummy.[2]

Online, put this technique to use by pausing before you post. Why are you adding that link to Facebook? Will it be valuable to the many people who will see it? Or are you just flashing a Prius-shaped gang sign to your pals? If it's the latter, keep it to yourself.

Tell a story

Shitty pictures of your food are all over the Internet. Sites like Instagram are loaded with photo after photo of lumpy goo. What you're *trying* to share is the joy you feel when the waiter delivers that beautifully plated pork chop. But your photo doesn't tell the story of that experience. Your photo rips away the delicious smell, the beautiful room, the anticipation of eating, and the presence of people you love.

Instead, think of your photo as a story. When people tell stories, they think about how to communicate the entirety of their experience to someone else. They set the stage, introduce characters, and give us a reason to care. Of course, that's hard to do in a single photo, but if you think in terms of story, could you find a better way to communicate your experience? How about a picture of the menu, or of your smiling dinner companions? Anything's better than the greasy puddles you have decided any human with access to the Internet should be able to see.

Expand your circles

Several years ago, my wife and I went on a long trip. We had saved a little money, and the places we were staying were cheap, so we could afford private rooms in every city but one. Guess where we made the most friends? In Budapest, where we were jammed into a big room with a bunch of folks, we were forced into situations we never would have sought out. I wouldn't have met Goran, the Marilyn Manson superfan who was fleeing the NATO bombing of Belgrade on a fake Portuguese visa. Or Kurt, the Dutch hippie who let us crash on his floor in Amsterdam. Stepping out of your social comfort zone can be painful, but it's one of the most rewarding things you can do.[3]

As you widen your social circle, work on your intellectual one as well. Expose yourself to new writers. Hit the Random Article button on Wikipedia. Investigate the bromides your friends chuck around Twitter like frisbees.

When you expand your social and intellectual range, you become more interesting. You're able to make connections that others don't see. You're like a hunter, bringing a fresh supply of ideas and stories back to share with your friends.

The Big Bore lurks inside us all. It's dying to be set loose to lecture on Quentin Tarantino or what makes good ice cream. Fight it! Fight the urge to speak without listening, to tell a bad story, to stay inside your comfortable nest of back-patting pals. As you move away from boring, you will never be bored.

LMY

---

1 Lots of books exist because of how boring you have made the Internet. Books like *The Information Diet* focus on the consumption side of things: how are we, your readers and friends, supposed to deal with the junk you keep sending us? Instead, I'd like to look at the supply side: if you were more interesting, then there would be less junk out there that we would have to deal with. MHL

2 You don't have to go back to the '70s to find good listeners. My friend Jesse Thorn is a great interviewer who also listens in an engaged way. Check out his show, Bullseye. Or if you'd like to shoot for something a bit more academic, BBC's *In Our Time* features great conversation led by another master, Melvyn Bragg. BDZ DQM

3 These folks make a great case for the potentially life-changing value of meeting new people: Nassim Taleb's *The Black Swan*, and Porter Gale's "Conversations with 4C." RDS GBC

A Ribbon Runs Through It

**When one sews one's own clothes,
the questions have a common thread.**

BY ERIN MCKEAN

"W"hen did you start sewing?" I'm asked, and I reply, "When I was 12," which is the truth, but the real question should be: "When did you start to love sewing?" The answer to that has actual documentary evidence, in the form of a snapshot, the kind that today makes you think "bad Instagram filter."

My friend N. and I are both about 15. We're grinning, with my braces on full display, as we hold up the ribbons we won at a summer Latin competition. (It is an *extremely* geeky picture.) I've been sewing for a couple of years, but only in fits and starts, with more unfinished, overambitious projects wadded up in the sew-

Appeared in
Issue 17,
May 23, 2013

ing closet than finished dresses. My mom made my dress, and my friend N. is wearing the dress I made from the same pattern.

We're on our way to the dance, and there will be cute boys there — cute boys who think it's awesome that N. and I kick ass at tests of Latin derivatives and are wearing slightly weird, obviously homemade dresses. This is one of the first times (if not the first time) that I realize life is for doing — and wearing — what makes me so happy in the company of like-minded folks.

Every new dress I make evokes that feeling again. In a new dress, anything can happen.

I like this dress, but I'm self-conscious about the patch pockets, which are not quite perfect.

How long is a piece of thread?

"How long does it take you to make a dress?" they ask. "Four hours if it's a pattern I've made before, a bit longer if it's something new or complicated or if there are a lot of buttonholes," is the hedge-filled answer, and sometimes these calculations are visible.

It just takes so long to drive to the mall or the department store or to wander down a street of little boutiques, so long to surf through favorite shopping sites, to check the daily-deal emails, so much time to try things on, to stand in line at the post office to return something. None of which are as enjoyable as the snip of the scissors through the fabric, the hiss of the iron pressing a seam flat, or even the held-breath suspense of checking to see if the zipper lined up right.

Four hours sewing late on a Sunday night, after everyone else has gone to sleep, in order to wake up and put on a new dress the next morning; five hours on a Saturday afternoon with rap music blaring as accompaniment to a tricky fitting problem; a three-hour marathon session cutting out several dresses at once, until my hands get sore and the podcast queue is empty. Plus the time spent browsing fabric sites over my breakfast, or running to the fabric store in the Mission in the middle of a project because the spool ran out of black thread with one last seam to go.

I don't sew to save time; I sew because I enjoy the time I spend sewing.

QGZ

Thank you for your support

"I love your dress! Is it vintage?" the clerk at that same fabric store asks me while cutting me three yards of lightweight twill with little black and gray heart-and-lightning-bolt amalgams on it. I'm daydreaming about what I'll make — a shirtdress? another Vogue 9929? — and so she asks me again.

"It's from a vintage pattern." I used a metal zipper, too, just to make it more vintage-y, so it's not a dumb question. I like this dress, but I'm self-conscious about the patch pockets, which are not quite perfect. I never get them exactly right. It took a few years, but I no longer respond automatically to dress compliments with an apology for its imperfections.

"Oh, but is the fabric vintage? It looks vintage."

"I bought the fabric in Japan, I think. Five or six years ago, so kinda vintage." Now she's cutting me four yards of bright pink seersucker plaid. It will look gorgeous (and feel marvelous, light, and billowy) as a big full skirt.

"Oh, yes, it looks Japanese." The print is little white, red, and brown birds on a mustard background, but I know what she means. (Japanese fabric is not all red chrysanthemums picked out in gold paint.)

On this particular Saturday afternoon of running errands, four people tell me they love this dress: the nice barista at Blue Bottle (who reads my blog, so that doesn't really count), that fabric cutter, the clerk who rings me up, and a woman who calls out to me on the street as she walks by with her friends: "I love your dress!"

My response is always the same: "Thank you very much."

I sew only to please myself, but (as happens with so many things) the more I like a particular dress, the more public approbation it receives. I don't think it's because my dresses are examples of exquisite craftsmanship (those wonky patch pockets!). It's because I look happy while wearing them.

I am not a billboard

"Where did you get that dress?" I like full skirts, bright colors, and loud prints (especially camouflage, alphabet prints, and bold stripes), but even my weirdest clothes can make me feel safely invisible in a way: it's almost impossible to tell how much they cost.[1]

When you make your own clothes you can opt out, to some extent, from participating in brand culture: there are no labels, no logos, no convenient short-hand ways for people to pigeonhole you by your clothes. You have to be dealt with as a special case; you are distinctively anonymous. Nobody knows where you bought that dress.

There is, of course, another way to escape fashion-branding hegemony. William Gibson outlines it in his description of Cayce Pollard in *Pattern Recognition*:

> CPUs. Cayce Pollard Units. That's what Damien calls the clothing she wears. CPUs are black, white, or gray, and ideally seem to have come into this world without human intervention.
>
> What people take for relentless minimalism is a side effect of too much exposure to the reactor-cores of fashion. This has resulted in a remorseless paring-down of what she can and will wear. She is, literally, allergic to fashion. She can only tolerate things that could have been worn, to a general lack of comment, during any year between 1945 and 2000. She's a design-free zone, a one-woman school of anti whose very austerity periodically threatens to spawn its own cult.

But dressing in CPUs (as cool as it is) means you miss out on color, most shapes, and flair. Unless you make *everything*, you have to participate in brand culture to some extent — but Cayce-like, I prefer what are now called "heritage" brands. These are brands that have had such long lives that they aren't tied to one time, place, or group: A Levi's jean jacket. Keds. Plain penny loafers and ballet flats, plain T-shirts, plain cotton cardigans.

Since most people's wardrobes are built of solid-colored separates, they want elaborate accessories, so the simple option (not printed, no logos, without snazzy buttons or "jewels," without ruffles or trim or decorative anything) is harder and harder to find, and almost always more expensive.

If I'm going to be judged by what I wear, I want what I wear to be as direct a reflection of myself as possible.

That said, I am not judging your jeans

"Do you ever wear...regular clothes?" These questioners come the closest to suspecting that "regular clothes" make me antsy and that my "fun hobby" might be near-as-dammit to obsessive-compulsive disorder. The joke answer is that since I started blogging about sewing, people feel disappointed if I'm conventionally clad. But the truth is that if I don't wear something I've sewn myself I feel disappointed and not myself; it's like I'm wearing a costume.

The last time I had to buy a pair of "regular" jeans was for a costume, a tease-a-colleague work prank. I went to the big flagship Levi's store in San Francisco's Union Square. I was probably the only person in the store wearing a skirt. It was just before closing and the stacks of jeans were tumbled and mauled, but I found a couple of pairs in what the label numbers said were my size.

They were not my size: waist and inseam measurements are necessary but not sufficient to find jeans that fit, and in my rush I had grabbed pairs from the wrong table. (Evidently I should have been looking for the Sir Mix-a-Lot table — "Oh my god. Becky, look at her butt!")

WPD

These are brands that have had such long lives that they aren't tied to one time, place, or group: A Levi's jean jacket. Keds.

I don't think it matters how good you feel about your body: trying on clothes that don't fit always makes you feel lacking in some way. (Why do we get mad at ourselves when clothes don't fit?) I make my clothes to suit my body, not my body to suit my clothes. This is not to say that I don't have "fat day" clothes, but sewing keeps me more in touch with (and forgiving of) those fluctuations. People sometimes tell me that they want to be at their "right" weight before they start sewing, but they have it backwards. When you wear clothes you really like that really fit, you feel better about your body and more inclined to take care of it.[2]

Another reason that wearing "regular" clothes sucks: 90 percent of ready-to-wear women's clothing has inadequate pockets or no pockets at all. What I carry in my pockets every day: my phone, one or two pens, a lipstick, my wallet, a 3.5×5.5 notebook, my keys. Sometimes I throw in my sunglasses case, my earbuds, and an extra light or two for my bike. (My pocket role model is Harpo Marx: someday I will fit a mannequin leg and a puppy in my pockets, with space left over for a sled.)

LSC

My daily haul wouldn't be that notable for a guy in a sports coat, but when I start pulling things out of my pockets in front of other women, their response is always the same: "I wish my clothes had pockets."

My hatred for the handbag-industrial complex probably verges on the irrational, but you can't tell me that the rise of the expensive-designer-handbag fetish and the lack of pockets in women's clothing are purely coincidental. Pockets are a feminist issue: how much more could women accomplish if we had the full use of both arms?

Not for sale

The most uncomfortable questions always circle around selling: "Do you ever sew for other people?" "Do you sell what you make?" "Could you make me something?" I always feel selfish saying, no, my clothes aren't for sale. Sewing professionally would turn my hobby into a job.

Professional work brings in all the worst parts of sewing: fitting, alterations, and slippery fabric. I don't want to sew corsets, wedding dresses, or even trousers. Besides, no one would want to pay what I'd need to charge to make a living at it.

There's a reason that all the clothes sold at the big retailers are made far away, by people making pennies an hour. My time costs me nothing; being my own sweatshop weirdly counts as entertainment. But the economics of sewing for other people just doesn't work.

If they look disappointed that I don't take on commissions, I try to sell them instead on the idea that they should try making their own clothes. It's not a case of Tom Sawyer and the whitewash; sewing is hugely interesting, fun, fulfilling, and creative, and it's not as hard as it seems. "If you can drive a car and follow a recipe, you can sew," I say. "You just have to be able to use an accelerator pedal, measure stuff, and follow instructions."

YouTube is crammed with videos that will show you how to do all the tricky things I had to learn from the *Reader's Digest Complete Guide to Sewing*. There are sites (like BurdaStyle and PatternReview.com) that host feedback on patterns, show off finished garments, and even run online classes. And there are even places that will rent you a sewing machine by the hour.

The hardest thing to describe, however, is the feeling of putting on something that is your idea made real. That reification is familiar to anyone who makes, whether coder, chef, knitter, brewer, or beyond. And the more practice you get in making your ideas real, the easier it is to have bigger and bigger ideas. I don't think I'd be working at a startup today if I hadn't started sewing as a kid.

Asked and answered

I don't really mind having these conversations, even the "will-you-make-me" ones, because talking about sewing is inherently pleasurable, and I will talk about sewing every chance I get. Traveling is an excuse to buy fabric; going to a wedding or giving a talk is an excuse to make a new dress. Heck, a sunny Tuesday is an excuse to make a new dress.

And it's good that I'm happy to answer these questions forever, because I can't imagine a future me who wouldn't want to spend her Saturday mornings flooring the sewing machine's pedal. When I plan for my inevitable old age, I think about what tech might keep me sewing. I'm thinking industrial exoskeletons, or probably a variation on 3D printing.

The "what" I sew might change — perhaps I'll get deep into tailoring, or asymmetric Japanese patterns, or printing my own fabric — but I never want to lose that 15-year-old's feeling that the world is a place for the exuberant indulgence of enthusiasm.

1 A typical dress for me costs anywhere from $10 to $75 in fabric, made from a pattern that costs anything from free (sometimes people send me their patterns so they can live out their lives in a happy place, like sending your cat or dog to a farm) to $20 or so. Add in another few dollars for notions (buttons, thread) — and completely ignore the thousand dollars or so in sewing equipment (sewing machine, $100 iron, scissors, and so on).

2 Even if you don't sew, it's hugely worthwhile to take clothing in for alterations. Buy garments that fit in the shoulders and bust and hips, and get the length and waist changed to suit you just as you are now.

Instant Memories

The Impossible Project has earned its name by re-inventing instant film for Polaroid cameras.

By MAARTEN MUNS

T he photographer and I ride up in a large and noisy elevator. Our chaperone points to the photographer's camera. "You should use a Polaroid camera in this building," she says. "This is still an old-fashioned digital one," I reply. She smiles and repeats my words softly and slowly. "An 'old-fashioned' digital camera. That's funny."

In Enschede, a town on Holland's eastern border with Germany, factories churned out textiles and other products from the early 19th century until the 1970s, when the last shut down due to competition from Asia. The Polaroid film factory was a late arrival, built in 1965 and shuttered by the firm in 2008. But a brightly colored phoenix rose almost immediately from the ashes, and the plant brims with energy today.

As digital photography and digital photo printing became increasingly affordable, demand for Polaroid film plummeted. The firm filed for bankruptcy in 2001, and the new entity that bought its assets decided in 2004 that instant film's future was dim. It stockpiled what it thought was enough chemicals to meet demand for new film for a decade, and dismantled its ability to make

Appeared in
Issue 12,
March 14, 2013

more. Film sold faster than expected, depleting reserves. Meanwhile, the new Polaroid began closing its factories as it tried to shift to putting its name on and making digital products. It stopped making instant cameras first, then film. The new Polaroid filed for bankruptcy in 2008.

That would have seemed to be the end for Polaroid film, even as the company assets were sold again and the name slapped on unrelated digital cameras and other products. The knowledge of thousands of workers across many decades was scattered. But the Enschede plant's closure contained the seeds of the return of an instant film, lacking just the Polaroid name.

They couldn't acquire the formulas, processes, or raw chemicals. Instead, the company had to re-invent Polaroid's magic with enormously fewer resources.

But that's Impossible

Florian Kaps, an Austrian entrepreneur, met André Bosman at the closing party for the Enschede factory in 2008. Bosman was the factory manager whose job it was to shut down the complex, while Kaps ran a Web site selling Polaroid products. Kaps and Bosman both loved Polaroid's instant film and decided to save this last factory and find a way to continue production. They both felt there was still a strong demand for this type of photographic magic.

Kaps contacted Polaroid with a plea to hand over its production secrets. "We have shut down," the regretful Polaroid manager replied. "What you want is impossible." That didn't deter them; rather, it was a call to action. Kaps and Bosman started the Impossible Project. They leased the Enschede building and bought many of the machines that made Polaroid film, but they couldn't acquire the formulas, processes, or raw chemicals. Instead, the company had to re-invent Polaroid's magic with enormously fewer resources.

One can find many accounts of this period of the Impossible Project's life (both before and during the launch of its film products in 2010), such as *Wired UK*'s lengthy feature from 2009. But outside of photo magazines and sites, precious little has been written since, even as Impossible has expanded production

HCX

Type http://magcode.me/ plus a blue code in the margin to visit the related Web page.

and continued to raise significant capital.

The firm says it shipped 500,000 packs of film in 2010, 750,000 in 2011, and nearly a million in 2012. Sales continue to climb. Capitalized initially with €1.2 million (about $1.6 million) from friends, family, and angel investors who went on to chip in an additional €3.5 million ($4.5 million) through 2011, the firm says it raised unspecified "significant funding" in 2012 for substantial expansion of its work. Impossible hosts project spaces in New York, Paris, and Japan. (Japan's Fujifilm continues to make its own instant products.) Its headquarters are in Vienna, but its main research and development efforts remain located in the old factory in Enschede.

On assignment for *The Magazine*, I visited the plant with a photographer in February 2013 to see how the Impossible Project had become entirely possible. We met Martin Steinmeijer, the project's chief chemist and a precise, enthusiastic, and hard-working man, like so many in this part of the Netherlands.

Steinmeijer takes us to a large room where dozens of developed instant photos lie on a table. Some are overexposed; some too dark. Steinmeijer explains, "These photos have been shot in a cold room in our lab on our new PX 100 black-and-white film. You can see that they have not developed the way they should in temperatures far below zero. Not a major problem in everyday use, but we have to fix it."

Steinmeijer is clearly a perfectionist. "Polaroid's production used to be fragmented," he tells me. "In this factory we mainly produced the chemical paste needed for the development of the film, and we manufactured the film packs. The negatives, the sheet material, and the pigments all came to us from the United States. We had no knowledge of the techniques whatsoever."

But in 2010, the project started developing instant films that can be used in almost every old Polaroid camera, like the Polaroid 600 and SX-70. The new media include both monochrome "silver" and full-color film, which rely on completely different techniques. Impossible says they even improved the old Polaroid qualities. The films have "never seen before color saturation, a completely new level of detail and sharpness, and overall stunning image quality," according to its press releases — and confirmed by reviews and my eyes.

I appreciate the fine, warm colors in these images as opposed to the hard, sharp prints that often come from a modern digital instant-print camera. Kirstin McKee, a London photographer, likes the film for its variation. McKee was recently featured on the Impossible Project's blog for photos she took on a trip to Crete. She says via email that she has found instant-film pictures appealing for a few years, and started "trawling eBay" to acquire Polaroid cameras to try out with the project's film.

McKee says Impossible's film "is a pleasing contrast from the reliable repeatability of digital imaging. Polaroids are, in other words, more like memories. They are unreliable, rose-tinted, and capricious, and their characteristic format is somehow inherently nostalgic."

Speeding up

The firm sells several varieties of film for about $3 an exposure, mostly in packs of eight. The price and variability of results mean the film currently appeals mainly to photographic artists rather than general consumers. A Flickr group for instant-film shooters gives a good sense of how Impossible's film (and the precious remaining Polaroid stock) is being used. But there are other drawbacks that Impossible must overcome before it can reach even a fraction of the mass audience that Polaroid once captured.

"Polaroids are more like memories. They are unreliable, rose-tinted, and capricious, and their characteristic format is somehow inherently nostalgic." — McKEE

"One of the most appealing aspects of old-style Polaroid photography is seeing your photo develop in a few minutes after shooting. This is a unique experience totally absent in modern digital cameras," Steinmeijer says. "But with our films it takes much too long for the picture to appear." He sounds worried.

Impossible's first films have two problems. After shooting, the negative behind the photo sheet remains very sensitive to light, and it has to be shaded the instant it comes out of the camera. The first half-second is critical, but an exposure must be kept out of the light for up to four minutes to be safe. On top of that, full development takes 10 to 20 minutes.

A new color-protection film, which has greater saturation as well, solves the problem of extreme light sensitivity, but still takes a long time to produce an image. (The monochrome film retains both issues, and the older color film is still sold.) The new film, released in late 2012, squeezes a layer of opacifier over the sheet

as it comes out of the camera. This layer, only about 0.1 millimeters thick, consists of protective titanium dioxide and indicator pigments, and protects against all but full sunlight.

The pigments decolorize (change from opaque to clear) in about half an hour after the negative has been developed and is no longer photosensitive. But the developing process requires just five minutes in the new film. Impossible is trying to narrow that gap. "It is a huge challenge to bring that back to exactly the time needed," Steinmeijer explains. "When your picture develops, you should be able to see the chemistry taking place in the palm of your hand. We are not that far yet. We are working very hard on this problem."

Of course, that may be part of the charm of Impossible's film at this stage of the market's development. Photographer McKee notes that "instant" pictures have a process all their own: "It does not appear, immediately and flawlessly, on the camera's screen, but takes its own sweet time to develop, often in unpredictable ways."

Shake it like a smartphone

Today, Impossible is the only company producing instant film for original Polaroid cameras. But the project is not only about reviving Polaroid instant photography. Last year it developed its first new hardware concepts. In an office at the Enschede factory, the firm showed me a prototype of a fascinating invention called the Impossible Instant Lab, which captures the image on an iPhone screen onto instant film.

Just launch the Impossible-designed app and select a picture. Place the iPhone in a cradle on top of an expandable hood connected to the newly designed film-processing unit, which contains mechanical gears that process and eject the photo after shooting. Then open the shutter. The app flashes the picture on the iPhone screen just long enough to expose the film. The sheet rolls out of the processing unit, and you can see an "analog" iPhone image develop in the palm of your hand. Just like old times, but with a digital twist.

The Impossible Project used crowdfunding to raise the funds for Instant Lab. It had a target of $250,000 and raised nearly $560,000 on Kickstarter. The funds will allow it to go from a working prototype into mass production, with an expected price of $300. Although Instant Lab was promised to be available to Kickstarter backers in February, the usual delays between early prototypes and the production line have pushed delivery back to no earlier than April.

The Impossible Project used crowdfunding to raise the funds for Instant Lab. It had a target of $250,000 and raised nearly $560,000.

But the Instant Lab isn't a single project. The film-processing unit that's part of it will form the basis of new instant-film cameras already in the design phase. "If you place a lens on the front of the processing unit together with a mirror, then you have a Polaroid camera," one of the researchers explains. He takes a Polaroid camera from the 1970s out of a glass case. The two designs are basically the same.

It is never easy to re-invent a 20th-century success story from scratch. And in a time when everything needs to be small, fast, and portable, will a mass market for instant-film photography once again develop? Steinmeijer and the rest of the dedicated team in Enschede believe it will.

"Surprisingly, it turns out that our consumers are also youngsters, who have never been familiar with Polaroid anyway. Apart from artists, we also want to make our instant film practical for people who just want to take a quick picture. Instant film is such a wonderful, quick, and easy-to-use product. That is the reason we think we can re-conquer the large group of customers Polaroid once had," he says.

Photographer McKee has a simpler answer: "A Polaroid links me physically to the past in a way a digital image never could."

How to Make a Baby

The path to parenthood isn't always straightforward.

By GINA TRAPANI

Appeared in
Issue 2,
Oct. 25, 2012

Choosing a sperm donor is a little bit like setting up an Xbox avatar. You begin by deciding on the ethnicity, hair color, and eye color of the fellow whose sperm you'd like to combine with your egg to make your baby. Then you enter that criteria into a sperm-bank search engine, which returns a list of matching anonymous males who passed rigorous genetic tests and filled out detailed questionnaires. Finally, you pore through each donor profile, considering things like his height, weight, build, SAT scores, family medical history, sexual orientation, whether or not he has moles, the shape of his nose and mouth, and in some cases, his baby photo or voice sample.

Our sperm bank has a Web-based form to search its database. When I use tools like this, as a developer I can't help but think about the coders behind it. Did the people who wrote this HTML really consider their end-users? Did they visualize the lesbians, the single women, the aspiring parents who had everything lined up except viable sperm? Did they imagine the tension, the hope, the bizarre feeling of picking out the genetic material to make your baby online, the same way you'd shop for computer parts?

In my Web browser, I scroll down a page of search results, clicking the

Illustration by Simmons Ardell

mouse wheel here and there to open potential donor profiles in background tabs.

My parents, devout Catholics, conceived me by accident. They had agreed that they were finished having children after their third, my sister. They got rid of all the baby clothes, the car seat, the toys, and the crib. Our family was big, the house was full, and they were happy — until seven years later, when the rhythm method failed them. News that Mom was pregnant with me was met with both joy and concern. Dad worried about space, tuition, and parenting stamina. They bought all the baby stuff anew. Later, they'd tell the story of how I was a surprise, and I heard the undertones. They loved me so much, but my late-in-life arrival was stressful.

My wife and I have been discussing having a child for seven years. Unlike the path to parenthood of our heterosexual counterparts, ours is not straightforward. We debate whether or not we're ready, which one of us should carry, who our donor should be, where we would adopt from. In the meantime, our biological clocks tick and tock in tandem, louder every year. Forty looms. We either have to make a move or get a cat.

You picked a good one

I show up at the sperm bank, credit card in hand. We've decided on a donor, and my wife is going to carry. She's older than I am, so she gets first dibs. If it doesn't work, I'll try. Redundant uterus backup! I've never purchased sperm before and I'm nervous. I try not to think about the men who have come through this place, in the back rooms stocked with sterile cups and pornography.

When she sees the donor code, the nurse behind the counter lights up. "Oh! You picked a good one," she tells me, winking. "I know him, and I really like him." Either she's a great salesperson, or our superior search skills unearthed a gem. I choose to believe the latter. Still, it's weird that this stranger knows our child's sperm donor, and we won't.

The vials of sperm come frozen in a tank, which they roll out on a small hand truck. In the parking lot, I strap the tank into the passenger seat of my car with the seatbelt. Driving across town to the fertility center, we get stuck in traffic — me and the sperm that I hope will make my kid. I glance over at it. "You've got to swim, baby, swim!" At times like these, I feel like I'm co-starring in a bad sitcom about lesbians having kids.

Almost half a dozen attempts at artificial insemination fail. Every month is an emotional cliff. After each procedure we leave the fertility center high on hope. Two weeks later, not pregnant, we're crushed. I'm ready to bring in our backup uterus, but my wife wants to keep trying.

Our doctor upgrades us to in vitro fertilization (IVF), which is more expensive, more invasive, and more effective. At home, my wife shoots herself up with hormones and downs prenatal vitamins. At the hospital, they extract her eggs. I'm beside myself. I'm in awe of what a good mother my wife already is, enduring endless exams, painful injection bruises, and a collection of daily pills, always calm and without complaint. Every night, I try not to stick her in the wrong place with the needle.

The first "test tube baby" was born in 1978. I was three years old. I can't believe that within my lifetime, a complex procedure like IVF is available to regular people (with enough savings) like my wife and me. I think about all the scientists and doctors and technologists whose lives' work might help create my child. I try to focus on my gratitude instead of worry.

At the lab, the embryologist injects the sperm directly into my wife's eggs.

"The embryos like it dark," our doctor says, as the nurse dims the lights. I'm not sure how a handful of cells that have just begun to divide could possibly have a lighting preference, but I just nod. The embryologist brings into the room our fertilized egg, which she has loaded from a petri dish into a syringe. The doctor injects our embryo into my wife. We all hold hands and have a moment of silence, willing the baby to find a place to attach, grow, and thrive.

We binded her with science

Our baby girl was born on September 18, 2012. She looks just like my wife, which means I get to fall in love again with a new iteration of the most important person in my life.

My conception was an accident, but my daughter's was the opposite. When she grows up, she will hear how her moms conceived her in their minds years before she was conceived in a lab. She will find out that we went to the greatest emotional, financial, and medical lengths possible to bring her into this world. She will learn of the complicated and incredible medical technology that helped make her, and how lucky we were to have access to it.

When she understands all of that, she will be proud to be a test tube baby. She will know how much we wanted her, our precious result of a mad science experiment gone wonderfully right.

Light Motif

**A pinhole cap finally brings infinite focus and
undistorted images to digital cameras.**

By DAVID ERIK NELSON

ustin Lundquist was watching TV in 2009 and saw a commercial for one of the first cameras built around the new Olympus/Panasonic "Micro Four Thirds" system. These are high-end digital cameras with interchangeable lenses, and are similar to digital single-lens reflex (DSLR) designs, which show precisely through the viewfinder what the camera captures via its lens.

PJW

The design goal with Micro 4/3 was to make a professional camera significantly more compact than any DSLR. What got Lundquist on the phone to his soon-to-be business partner — another Chicago-based photographer, Ben Syverson — was a word that probably didn't impress anyone else watching that ad: "mirrorless."

In order to shrink the camera body, Olympus/Panasonic did away with the

angled reflex mirror at the heart of any high-quality camera. The mirror allows a shooter to see, via a tiny viewfinder, what the lens sees. Because the design had a compact camera body and no mirror in the way, Syverson and Lundquist (who happens to be my brother-in-law) realized that they could remove the lens entirely and place a usable pinhole within a few millimeters of the camera's CCD sensor.

Lundquist, a freelance photographer, has experimented with pinhole cameras for decades. The mirrorless guts of the Micro 4/3 allowed him to finally see beyond the necessity of hacking together his own little digital pinhole camera: He could offer a pinhole add-on to an existing body. The Pinwide, a "pinhole cap," is the result. It transforms any Micro 4/3 camera into an honest-to-god ultra-wide-angle digital pinhole point-and-shoot.

A super brief foray into physics

A lens creates a sharp image by gathering photons and directing them toward its focal point. Collecting more light reduces exposure times and noise, creates brighter images, and increases detail. But a lens bends the light it gathers; the image it casts is not true to the object. The most obvious example of this is the barrel distortion created by a wide-angle lens.

You and I both know that no architect designed a roofline with that curve, and no masons tried to build it that way. This image is grossly distorted, but every image coming through a lens has at least subtle distortions corrected by optics and electronics.

Strong distortion from a fisheye lens. **Photo by Wade Patrick Brooks**

RBH

A pinhole camera creates no such distortion because it never alters the path of any photon. Instead, it sharpens an image by massively reducing the number of photons that reach the image plane. Blurriness, in part, is caused by a "point-to-patch" correlation between object and image, where photons striking a given point on the object scatter at slightly different angles and thus strike over an area of the image plane, rather than at one point. By blocking these stray photons, the pinhole brings us closer to an ideal point-to-point correlation between object and image.

The closer you bring a pinhole to the sensor, the smaller it can be. A smaller pinhole blocks more stray photons, and thus yields a sharper image. Shorter distances between pinhole and sensor yield a wider viewing angle, because the entire cone of light cast by the pinhole falls onto the tiny CCD sensor, which has about half the area of a US postage stamp. The result is a super-wide-angle field of view with no lens distortion.

Appeared in
Issue 10,
Feb. 14, 2013

A pinhole camera creates no such distortion because it never alters the path of any photon. Instead, it sharpens an image by massively reducing the number of photons that reach the image plane.

Go build a camera

It's not hard to make a simple non-mechanical, non-digital pinhole camera. Grab a cardboard box for its body. An oatmeal canister or other tube is good, because you want it lightproof and any joint is an opportunity for a leak. While you're digging through the recycling bin, keep an eye out for an old pie tin or soda can.

Cut a small square hole in the side of your would-be camera body, roughly midway down the length of the tube. Don't worry about making it perfect. This isn't rocket science; it's photography.

Spray-paint your box and its lid matte black, inside and out. If the lid or bottom is translucent, back it with a circle of thicker cardboard or plastic before painting. Once that paint dries, you're just a few minutes away from taking pictures. Cut a piece of aluminum a half inch or so bigger than your square hole. Drill a hole in its center with a pin, then tape that little square of aluminum over your tube's little square hole. Electrical tape is handy here; you want this to be light tight.

Want to take a picture? That's where things are trickier today than they were once upon a time when Kodak was solvent and every school or rec center had a fully stocked darkroom. Those days are gone, but if you have access to a darkroom, then you're going to go into that darkroom, slide a piece of photo paper into the back of the tube, seal it up, cover your pinhole with your thumb, and head outside. Find something well-lit that you want to photograph, point your camera in its general direction, and remove your thumb for a few dozen seconds. Stay still! Don't even breathe!

Despite the enduring allure of pinhole, no decent analog or digital pinhole camera or accessory has ever come to market.

Cover that hole back up, head back to the darkroom, pull out the paper, develop it, and — pow! You've got a negative version of what you photographed. Want a positive version (that is, one where the shadows are black and the light is white)? Clamp another sheet of photosensitive paper on top of your negative image, expose them to really bright light for a good long while, and then develop that second paper. Voilà!

Even a pinhole evangelist like my brother-in-law acknowledges that this is a pain in the ass.

"The reason it sucks is because you're stuck being near a darkroom, because it's a one-shot thing: You put one piece of 5-by-7 [inch photographic] paper into the oatmeal can, you go out somewhere relatively close, you go back into the darkroom and process it and see how it looks. If you want to take another picture, you load it while you're in the darkroom and go out again. So it's simple to build and to use, but it's not practical for taking a bunch of shots out and about."

Despite the pain-in-the-assery of it all, pinhole cameras offer certain advantages that keep us coming back. First and foremost is that a pinhole camera has no lens, which means an infinite depth of field with no lens distortion. In other

words, everything from the pinhole to infinity is equally in focus. Set your camera in a meadow and take a picture of the clear sky; each blade of grass is just as sharp as the moon.

But the most readily recognized hallmark of pinhole photography is the natural vignetting. This is the fairly pronounced circular light falloff from a bright center to shadowed edges.

A dearth of commercial pinhole gear

Despite the enduring allure of pinhole, no decent analog or digital pinhole camera or accessory has ever come to market. This isn't to say that there's been no attempt at pro-grade pinhole gear, just that the results have been disappointing.

Despite their complete lack of experience in engineering, industrial design, or physics, Lundquist and Syverson immediately realized why: most pre-digital interchangeable-lens SLRs and their electronic DSLR descendants use the same method (developed in the late 19th century): allowing a single objective lens to serve as both the viewfinder and the "taking" lens.

SLRs and DSLRs have a flip-up mirror mounted just behind the lens. When you squint through the viewfinder, that mirror is resting at a 45-degree angle between the lens and your eyepiece, which has its own fixed 45-degree-angle mirror — it's like a periscope — beaming whatever the camera sees directly to your eye. When you press the shutter release, the little mirror flips up out of the way and the shutter cycles, exposing the film. Then the mirror drops back into place and you're back to viewing. DSLRs may use an image sensor instead of film, but they otherwise maintain all of an old film SLR's internal mechanics.

This clever arrangement of flip-up mirrors is fine if you're using a lens, but replacing the lens with a pinhole proves entirely unworkable: the reflex mirror forces a huge gap between the pinhole aperture and the sensor (or film). At that distance, the pinhole itself must be made larger to allow more light to pass through. The result is a blurrier image that overspills the sensor, and is thus cropped square. This is totally unacceptable to guys who really care about pinhole.

Mirrorless cameras opened the opportunity, but making a precision product — one that performs consistently — is a far cry from hacking something together from recyclables and tape. The real challenge is the pinhole itself. First of all, that hole has to be as smooth and round as possible. Additionally, you want the material surrounding the pinhole to be thinner than the diameter of the hole — otherwise, light bouncing off the interior surface of the passage scatters unpredictably on the image plane, blurring the picture. The Pinwide's design calls for a pinhole less than a third the size of a period on a printed page; you aren't going to get that in molded plastic, or even by popping pins through pie tins.

Committed non-digital pinhole hobbyists buy thin metal foil that's been custom micro-drilled, or even laser-drilled. While this can have good results photographically, the cost is prohibitive: at $30 a pop, using either method would have doubled the price of the Pinwide.

Then Lundquist and Syverson discovered chemically etched aperture grids made for electron microscopes. These are minuscule holes burned through tiny circles of ultra-thin vapor-deposited foil. They're produced using an industrial process and can be bought only in bulk; totally impractical for a lone hobbyist monkeying around on his own, but a fraction of the cost of a manually drilled pinhole aperture once you do the per-unit math. And they take awesome pictures.

Signal and noise

As our tools become cheaper, cleaner, and crisper, we tend to grow nostalgic for the old "noisy" things of the past — the roar of a guitar overdriving an underpowered amp, the smeary Polaroid colors imitated by Instagram filters. I suggest to Lundquist that the Pinwide, which introduces the flat, wide angle and vignetting of yore to high-resolution digital photography, is one more example of our tendency to make yesterday's noise into today's signal.

Lundquist sets me straight: Yes, the software-based "pinhole" effects take a clear digital image — albeit one distorted by a glass lens — and further muck it up with filters, masks, and circular cropping. But the Pinwide is "just showing more of the image through to the dark edge where it's falling off, instead of cropping out what's naturally there." Any other camera configuration, from a junk-shop toy 35mm point-and-shoot to a $6,000 Canon EOS-1D X with all the trimmings, discards much of the large, circular image captured by its lens, preserving only the sharp, bright square at the center.

An actual pinhole photograph, analog or digital, is "a straight image that's being captured with just the light and the sensor," with nothing that intervenes. All you see is what's there, and you see it more and more clearly as you block out more and more of that stray light.

Afterword *As of early 2014 Ben and Justin — as Wanderlust Cameras — continue to sell the Pinwide pinhole cap, and they are on the cusp of releasing an affordable, ultra-portable large-format 4x5 film camera, the Travelwide.*

RBH

1 Amateur analog cameras, on the other hand, usually use a separate low-quality lens for the viewfinder – a sorta crappy version of the classic "twin-lens reflex" design – while   QBX   cheaper digital cameras use either this approach or low-resolution electronic viewfinders that pull an image from the CCD.

WOOD
STOCK

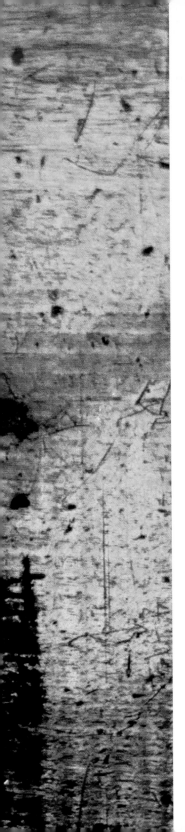

A once-obscure bit of printing history on the shores of Lake Michigan finds rekindled interest.

BY JACQUI CHENG

T he remnants of the Hamilton district in Two Rivers, Wisconsin — the former head-quarters of the country's largest producer of wood type in a town that once hummed with manufacturing — now largely sits quiet. The industrial building housed two last bits that came out of over 100 years of wood manufacture: a laboratory furniture operation, and the Hamilton Wood Type Museum. Save some old business cards scattered on the ground, the factory is empty.

Thermo Fisher Scientific, the descendant owner of Hamilton Wood Type Manufacturing and its buildings in Two Rivers, announced abruptly in 2012 that it would shut down its furniture division in Two Rivers. The museum was forced to move, and found a space a few blocks away. Now relocated and only recently chugging back to life, its unofficial motto is unchanged: "Preservation through use." The museum houses one of the few remaining shops in the world that can produce wood type, a mainstay for a century in the production of many kinds of printed work.

Like vinyl records, the sales of which have climbed back into the millions a year, wood type

Appeared in
Issue 20,
July 4, 2013

appears to be getting its groove back. A branding and exposure makeover for the museum, combined with the rapid rise of maker and crafts movements, have helped wood type carve out a new space.

Wood type has kept its appeal even as the born-digital generation starts to take charge of the world, maybe because members of that demographic have become aware of what they are missing. Current museum director Jim Moran says he can't teach enough traditional letterpress classes to satisfy demand. He believes if he had more time to carve new wood type, he would be able to sell every last piece.

Hamilton came up with his own style: cutting the characters out and gluing them to blocks of wood. The process was cheap but effective.

Type-cast

BTL

From Gutenberg's day to the early 1800s, movable type was cast in metal; wood blocks were used primarily for illustrations. Then in 1827, Darius Wells disrupted the industry by coming up with a way to mass-produce wood type for the large letter sizes that had begun to be desirable for advertising and newspaper headlines. This had numerous advantages over metal type, which was expensive to cast at such sizes, remarkably heavy, and susceptible to warping before it was cool.

Wood, on the other hand, was relatively cheap, light, and resilient, and could be carved with smooth surfaces. Wells released the first known wood type catalog just a year later, a move that led wood type to share the market with metal for almost 150 years.

In Two Rivers in 1879, James Edward Hamilton began working at a chair- and table-making factory as a lathe operator. Hamilton's friend Lyman Nash, then editor of the *Two Rivers Chronicle*, felt Hamilton's skills could be put to better use — namely, to carve letters for a poster he was printing on a tight deadline. Nash knew he could never get type delivered fast enough from the East Coast, where all other type was made, so he asked Hamilton to carve something — anything — he could use to get the poster done on time.

"Hamilton didn't know anything about type," Moran says. "He didn't see the future of it or anything like that. He was simply helping out a friend."

With no background in type carving, Hamilton came up with his own style: cutting the characters out and gluing them to blocks of wood. The process was cheap but effective — so much so that Hamilton found himself making more and more type for Nash's posters. Hamilton's hand-carved type evolved to the point where he thought he could turn it into a business, and in 1880, he did.

"Hamilton's business grew at such a rate that, as competition will do, some people were forced out of the market. Others simply sold to Hamilton because it was the easiest thing to do," Moran says of Hamilton's sudden success in the typemaking industry. The company's rapid growth can be attributed to the fact that every time he acquired a competitor's fonts and techniques, Hamilton would refine his own carving methods. (Hamilton also made type cabinets to store metal and wooden types, first from wood and later from steel.)

One of his most notable acquisitions was the William H. Page Wood Type

ZCQ

BJH

Company. "When Hamilton bought out Page, he switched to Page's way of making type, which was to make it out of a solid block of maple wood," explains Moran, adding that Wisconsin and much of the Midwest has a vast maple supply. "He kept buying out competitors and refining his techniques, and suddenly he had the entire market."

Indeed, it took only 11 years for Hamilton to dominate the wood typemaking industry; by the turn of the century, nearly all of Hamilton's competition had been either absorbed or eliminated. Hamilton had become the king of wood type in the United States without ever intending to do so.

Fossilized remains

Hamilton's manufacturing company stopped cutting its own type more than a hundred years later, in 1985. Moran calls this "way late," considering that Apple's first Macintosh computer was released in 1984. By then, demand for traditional type and typesetting was understandably limited, as computers were quickly revolutionizing type and design. Type enthusiasts prepared for the death of wood type and kept trying to buy Two Rivers patterns for private collections.

"Each piece needs a template, and you'd have all these pallets of these gorgeous patterns that were collected over time," Moran says. "That was all about to be sold, and that's when the Two Rivers Historical Society stepped in to create the Hamilton Wood Type Museum."[1]

In addition to the Hamilton museum, which opened in 1999, the rural industrial town also boasts a farm museum just a few streets away, which is not far from the historical ice cream parlor, tap room, and ballroom, all preserved thanks to the historical society.

But the Hamilton museum was unique in that Hamilton Manufacturing, long since sold to a new owner (the product of another ancient firm merged with a newer one), allowed the museum to coexist in the same historical factory building in Two Rivers, giving an extra hat tip to the museum's heritage.

It took only 11 years for Hamilton to dominate the wood typemaking industry; by the turn of the century, Hamilton's competition had been largely absorbed or eliminated.

"I think they initially saw the museum as more of a local thing that people from the area would like to visit," notes Moran.

But what made Hamilton's wood type collection so great also put it at odds with the location. "You can only find so many volunteers, particularly when they have no experience with the industry," says Moran. There wasn't nearly enough regional interest to suitably maintain the collection. (Some former workers acted as volunteers in the museum's early days, and a few have continued to donate their expertise. But the youngest worker when the wood-type operation shut down is well over 50 today.)

The historical society eventually appointed a director with a design background to help get the museum on track. But because the director had no background in traditional printing, neither Hamilton's equipment nor his collection was getting any use. The warehouse began stacking up with type, which was quickly becoming unusable thanks to leaks and poor ventilation rotting the wood.

"You couldn't come in and use the stuff. There were no regulations," says Moran. Only a few years after it opened, "It seemed like the place was just about ready to close."

"By 2003, it became clear that they were going to need a way to tell their story in a way that a couple paragraphs on a cool Web site wasn't going to." — BILL MORAN

A branding makeover

Jim Moran's brother Bill, a designer and printer, had been volunteering at Hamilton since 2001 and made it his personal goal to try to give Hamilton more exposure. "I was just completely blown away that I grew up 40 miles away from this thing I'd never heard of until I had been a practicing designer for 10 to 15 years," Bill Moran says of his interest in the museum. "Then I realized what they needed was good marketing."

Bill, a digitizer of old fonts, was a link between eras. He was a computer guy, but taught a printing history class at the University of Minnesota. In 2002, he began to push ideas on how to increase Hamilton's exposure to the world without changing its heart: the preservation, study, and use of wood-type letterpress printing. That began with a Web site, and then a book: *Hamilton Wood Type: A History in Headlines*.

"No one was talking about the place, and no one was really marketing the museum," Bill Moran says. "There were a handful of printers from around the country going there and making beautiful type, but by 2003, it became clear

that they were going to need a way to tell their story in a way that a couple paragraphs on a cool Web site wasn't going to." Bill is now the museum's artistic director.

The book was a success, at least in the design community. In 2008, Jim Moran, who had grown up in his family's printing business, took over as the new director of the museum. He had become enthralled with its history with the help of his brother's book. Then in 2009, Kartemquin Films released *Typeface*, an independently produced documentary about the Hamilton museum and its challenges. The film toured the world with numerous film festivals, painting for filmgoers what seemed to be a bleak picture of the museum's assumed fate.

"The film director told me the museum looked 'too sad' when I took him around," Jim says of his days spent with the film crew. "It looked like the place was dying. And that was accurate, too, but it's one of those things that makes the resurgence even more incredible."

Community revitalization

Once the film was released on DVD, iTunes, and Netflix, the messages began pouring in. Jim would roll in to work to find 10 new emails from Australia after a showing of *Typeface*. Then 15 new Facebook friends from Norway. Then a couple of visitors from Germany would show up. Suddenly, global interest in the Hamilton Wood Type Museum looked to be trending upward.

"The film helped us an incredible amount," says Jim. That same year, with Bill's help and connections to the design industry, Jim began offering letterpress workshops. He wanted to make Hamilton into more than just a museum, and felt that in order to best appreciate the craft, the equipment and collection had to be in active use. Much to his surprise, the workshops became a wild success.[2]

"I began to get wonderful interns from Australia and England and Germany," Jim says, highlighting the diversity of those interested in learning more about wood type. Few even knew how to make their way to Hamilton's rural

Museum assistant director Stephanie Carpenter

home — "I know how to get to Chicago, but how do I get to Two Rivers from there?" they would ask Jim — but they began coming in droves anyway.

Jim eventually found himself teaching a group of senior designers from Nike, and the museum even ended up partnering with Target to do a line of fall clothing that was designed by and licensed from the Hamilton museum. For nearly half a year, 1,755 Target retail stores sold clothing emblazoned with images from the Hamilton museum.

The exposure helped the museum staff feel like they were finally building mind-share among modern designers. Amidst this growing interest, Thermo Fisher Scientific announced that they were moving out of their industrial building in Two Rivers, evicting the museum and leaving it to fend for itself. Bill says that wasn't in itself bad, as the building had gone to pot: it had severe leaking and no heat. "We had the nation's largest collection of wood type and couldn't protect it," he says.

The current owners shifted the eviction date around, and zoning issues for the new location also caused worries. "There were so many unknowns as to whether they could come knocking on any given day saying we had to be out in a week. That kind of thing could have been ruinous," Bill recalls.

Branching out

By the time the new location was settled — with help from the town — in late 2012, "We ended up having about six months to bring in 1,500 hours of volunteer time, a phenomenal outpouring of money and hours to help us make this move," Bill says.

Even after the staff finished moving the massive collection, unpacking and re-organizing 26 semi-trucks' worth of pallets, they still had not reopened the space to the public when I visited in early June 2013. The enormous warehouse was only unpacked enough for the staff and volunteers to begin making their very first prints at the new location.

Jim, assistant director Stephanie Carpenter, and a group of volunteers were printing posters for an upcoming conference in San Francisco. There, they'd be showcasing some commissioned work for a client and giving talks to industry professionals about the museum and workshops. "We just can't keep up. Demand for our work — and the workshops — is huge," Jim says.

Indeed, part of the appeal of taking one of the $125 workshops at Hamilton is the ability to create art in practically any style using vintage equipment that's still in active use. Those who participate in the workshops end up creating 20 to 25 prints of their own throughout the day.

Moran thinks it's no coincidence that the uptick in participation in crafts and the do-it-yourself approach that has percolated back into culture has had a positive correlation with the revival of letterpress. Attendance at the workshops, he says, includes people who have been in the industry for a long time, but the bulk of participants are college-age graphic design students.

As that demographic continues to keep Hamilton afloat, Jim Moran now welcomes the trend with open arms. In fact, 27-year-old Carpenter only recently completed her master's degree in graphic design at Indiana University, representing a new wave of young people interested in practicing and maintaining the craft.

"There's a 30-year difference between us, so we come at this from different angles," Jim says. "But we both share a love of art and printing, and that's what makes our partnership unique. And she's a pretty good letterpress printer."

The museum's new location should be open to the public by August. The staff hopes to draw even more attention to its offerings through a vintage poster gallery, showcasing over 2,000 Globe printing plates from the 1920s through the 1960s, many of which were used to create successful posters for Ray Charles, Miles Davis, and historical musical venues. The Hamilton museum is now creating restrikes — or modern "mashups" — of that classic artwork.

NYG

Work cut out for it

One of Jim's plans to help keep the museum humming, and bring in a revenue stream, is to carve and sell new wood type. He's aware of only two other type-makers in the United States engaged in such work, and as a letterpress printing revival is underway, demand for the painstaking craft is high. The Hamilton museum has carved three sets of type in recent years, including one for a 600-year-old Native American language (called Lushootseed) that is on the verge of extinction.

WNC

SJX

Another was a new font by renowned type designer Matthew Carter. Carter, in his mid-70s and a recent MacArthur Foundation fellow, has a career that spans carving metal type as one of the last youth trained in that specialty, through very early work in computer-based typesetting, and into screen fonts for Web reading. If you've ever seen Verdana and Georgia, you know his work.

The museum commissioned a new face from Carter in 2003, but after working on initial designs cut into templates by a former Hamilton type cutter, they were stymied by limitations in that method. In 2009, the Morans revived the project and turned to a local shop that used a CNC (computer numeric controlled) router to cut the templates directly. Carter wrote,

> *On the day I arrived at Hamilton I picked up a piece of maplewood type and realised that it was exactly 50 years since a type of my design had been in a physical form that I could hold in my hand.*

Jim emphasizes that this is no easy (or cheap) process, but it's worth it for a quality product. It's the marriage of new and old methods, such as selling a rendition of Carter's face in digital form, that permeates the museum's revival. Despite the recent change of fortune, with a new building and a high level of outside interest, Jim and his team maintain an air of caution.

One of the main benefits to being located in the original Hamilton museum was free rent, with free light and utilities to boot — when they worked. Now, the museum holds the burden of those overhead costs. "We can support three salaries at this point and things are moving along very well," Jim said, "but we're still fragile."

"I could sell all the type we could make," Jim says. "We truly plan to get back into the business of making type. All we need are time and money."

---

1 Hamilton destroyed all its competitors' font patterns after each acquisition, a decision that still causes gnashed teeth among letterpress printers today when you mention it just as if they felt it had happened a few weeks before.

2 *Editor's note:* Your loyal editor took a half-day course from Jim and Bill in late 2010 in Seattle, which rekindled his love of letterpress printing from the 1980s. The two are infectious about their work, and Bill has a photographic memory for names and one's preferences for pie.

The Paste-Up

The smell of rubber cement is her madeleine.

By CAROLYN ROBERTS

Appeared in
Issue 20,
July 4, 2013

I remember the smell. It must be more than 20 years since I last experienced it, but it lingers in my nostrils still. It was sharp and strong, a scent reminiscent of petrol or turpentine in its pungency: thick, chemical, and unmistakably bad for you. It was called Cow Gum, and I loved it.

It was not, disappointingly, made of actual cow. Cow Gum was a rubber-based adhesive that my journalist mum used to do the paste-up, a long-forgotten task that must once have been the bane of editors' lives.

Mum ran a monthly magazine for women, all about rural life, agriculture, and home baking. I do not know why. My mum lived in cities her entire life. She rarely baked, and I have no evidence that she could tell one end of a pig from another. How she came to spend the last 20 years of her life working on a rural journal may well have been as much of a mystery to her as it is to me.

Illustration by Jacob Souva

Each month, Mum would sit down at the kitchen table with all of the articles for the next edition. They had been cut out to appear exactly as they would in the magazine: some were long and thin, some short and wide. Mum would paste each one onto a sheet of paper, ready to go to the printers. It must have been massively frustrating: you entered a profession because you loved words and language. But you ended up sticking a scrapbook together, scraping glue instead of ink from your fingers.

Words were what my mum did. She wrote on a blue typewriter, fingers battering the keys faster than anyone else I'd ever seen. Later, she typed on a computer keyboard just as quickly, but somehow it was never as thrilling as the clackety noise of the typewriter.

Growing up in a wordy family

In fact, words were the backbone of our family: my dad was a compositor, or typesetter as they are now more commonly called. Trained in the 1950s, Dad served a thorough and lengthy apprenticeship. It required six years of on-the-job training, attendance at college, and thrice-weekly night-school classes. Dad was trained to spot and correct mistakes before they were committed to type, engendering a lifelong devotion to correct grammar, spelling, and punctuation.

Growing up in a house so enamored with words and language had an effect on my childhood. I was never short of something to read, since publishers regularly sent my mum children's books for review. But we were never allowed to "read and run": the privilege of receiving a free book had to be paid for by writing a review, meaning that both my brother and I were published writers before we reached double figures.

And my goodness, those reviews had better be grammatically perfect. In our house, being below the age of 10 was not an acceptable excuse for poor spelling or — horror of horrors — an incorrectly deployed apostrophe. You might have written a story with a plot to rival Tolstoy's, but if you hadn't punctuated it accurately, you would be brutally mocked.

A compositor's training

Dad's training began when he was 15 and started work at an Edinburgh printing firm. He was allocated menial jobs until a place for an apprentice became free, as the unions had negotiated strict limits on the number of these junior workers that could be taken on at any one time. This protected the jobs of qualified union members by preventing firms from replacing them with cheaper trainees.

Once his apprenticeship was complete, my dad was officially a "journeyman," so called because in the past, qualified tradesmen would travel in search of work. The language of the printing trade is dense and hard to follow: when I interviewed Dad for this piece, I had to constantly ask for translations. Many of its phrases have their origins in religious orders, reflecting a time when monks were the custodians of the written word.

For example, when Dad served as the chief officer of his company's trade union branch, he was not, as he would have been anywhere else, a shop steward. Instead he was the father of the chapel, a phrase that baffled me as a child: I confusedly imagined him in a cassock, hearing the confessions of his workmates in between typesetting pages.

When Dad began his working life, the main form of printing was letterpress: the process of pressing inked hot metal type against paper. Although mechanical methods were already well established, compositors still had occasion to hand-set type, in the manner invented by Gutenberg in the 15th century. (Handsetting involved assembling metal letters in a composing stick to make words in a line.)

Each of these letters was stored in its own shallow drawer in a case, so the first task for an apprentice was to learn which drawer each letter was stored in. This was known as "learning the case." Some cases contained only lowercase letters, with the capital letters stored in another — from which the words "lowercase" and "uppercase" came.[1] Once the compositor had made up a complete page, it would be placed in a chase — similar to a photo frame — before going to press.

Until Dad retired in the late 1990s, his career changed in line with the industry's innovations. Initially he'd worked on a Monotype machine when not handsetting. Invented in the late 19th century, Monotype allowed much quicker typesetting, using perforations in paper to tell a separate casting machine which letters were required. (Such paper-tape systems were used to automate telegraphy with the invention of the Baudot code in the late 1800s, and then later to enter programs via a teletypewriter.)

But shortly after Dad qualified, Monotype and the similar Linotype machines — which allowed entry and casting of an entire line of text on a single machine — began to fall out of favor due to the advancement of photocomposition and lithographic offset printing.

Type http://magcode.me/ plus a blue code in the margin to visit the related Web page.

VRZ

The former exposed letters from glass plates onto film and then onto photo-sensitive paper, which was cut up for paste-up. The latter involved flexible printing plates (exposed from film negatives taken of the pasted-up type and halftoned images) that could be wrapped around a cylinder on a press, transferring the inked text and images first to rubber and then to paper.

The changing world

For both Mum and Dad, the irresistible advance of automation really began in the late 1980s. First the electronic typewriter replaced Mum's manual one that had juddered on our kitchen table for years. Soon afterward came the first personal computers with their desktop publishing packages, and suddenly the monthly paste-up was an anachronism. For a tiny magazine like Mum's, this new technology allowed work to be done more efficiently without affecting staffing levels simply because only three people worked there in the first place: there wasn't any dead wood to cut.

Things were different for Dad. Printing had been a highly individual and labor-intensive business. Once letters could be transferred to paper simply by depressing a few keys, whole battalions of proud and skilled journeymen became redundant, both conceptually and literally.

For my dad, now working at a national newspaper, it was clear that this was a game-changer. Dad's job shifted from laying out print using skills passed down over the centuries to simply pasting up pieces of paper, much as Mum used to do. Salaries were cut, and finally the paper's compositors were let go.

When Dad entered the printing trade in the middle of last century, his family confidently expected it to provide him with reliable employment all the way to retirement. Technological advances shattered those expectations and sent Dad back to night school at the age of 58 to learn how to use a Mac.

You'd expect Dad to be bitter about the computers that robbed him of his profession. He is not. My 76-year-old father uses Twitter to get updates on the condition of his local golf course, regularly Skypes my brother in Australia, and comments on photos of my baby daughter on Facebook.

No Luddite, he says that Macs actually returned some of the skill to the job of typesetting, allowing text to be formatted and manipulated in ways reminiscent of the old hot-metal days. He told me, "It is incredible now, looking back, to know that all the fonts, typecases, and chases (not forgetting the Monotype machines and casters used to do the typesetting) once found in those caserooms are all contained in one Apple Mac."

Looking back and looking forward

On a recent trip to the National Museum of Scotland, Dad and I came across an exhibit in the main hall. It was a printing press of the kind on which Dad had created proofs for checking over six decades ago. It was a very visual reminder that the skills he learned back in the 1950s have literally passed into history.

In the basement of the grand newspaper offices where Dad once worked, the massive thundering printing presses fell silent long ago. The unions, once belligerent and powerful, were broken and discarded by Rupert Murdoch in the decisive Wapping battles. The days of the kitchen-table publisher like my mum and the dedicated specialist like my dad have tumbled into antiquity.

So should we mourn their passing or give thanks for their obliteration? Print in Mum and Dad's day was a messy, dirty, tiring business. Today's technology is far more efficient and has opened up the world of publishing to anyone with a laptop and something to say.

What's more, in the days before tablets I'd never have seen a publication like *The Magazine*. It's produced in the United States, I'm all the way in Scotland, and our paths would likely never have crossed. Now I can read whatever interests me, regardless of where it is created.[2]

But I can't help being nostalgic for the old days. There is no longer much physical work associated with the printing process. The children of today's journalists and printers don't watch magazines being assembled by hand or conjure fanciful images of paper being branded by metal type blazing with heat. They'll never hear the terrifying roar of a room full of printing presses. And nevermore will children grow up with an unhealthy love for the smell of Cow Gum.

VCC

1 In America, upper- and lowercase letters were mixed in a California Job Case, an American invention for easier transportation of type to different locations.

2 *Editor's note:* We are largely produced in a basement in a home office located directly beneath a kitchen table on the main floor.

Icecapades

The clearer the ice, the smoother the melt.

By ALISON HALLETT

Appeared in
Issue 10,
Feb. 14, 2013

High-end cocktail bars spend a lot of time trying to replicate drinks that your average 19th-century sot took for granted. The methods used by bartenders in those days have little in common with your average present-day dive bar booze-slinger. Former Oregon Bartenders Guild president Dave Shenaut, who currently manages the bar at Portland's Raven & Rose, ticks off a list of reasons for the cocktail's 20th-century decline: rapid industrialization, mass production of booze and other bar ingredients, and the rise of processed food.

The death knell came in the 1980s, when calorie-counting, convenience-happy patrons didn't care a whit for interesting drinks. From a bartending standpoint, it was "vodka and four cans of mixers," he says morosely.

Over the past 15 years or so, though, "bartenders started looking at every element of the cocktail," explains bartender Sean Hoard of Portland's Teardrop Lounge. That includes small-batch booze, fresh-squeezed juice, handcrafted bitters and syrups, and all the tricks and techniques that would have made up an old-time bartender's arsenal. But the least obvious return has been a specialized kind of ice.

Photo by Pat Moran

If you've got ice cubes in your freezer, pull one out and take a look. More than likely, it's got a cloudy, feathered center. This cloudiness is caused by a few things, most notably impurities in your water and air bubbles trapped in the cube. They gather toward the center because ice freezes directionally: that is to say, if cold is applied to the surface of a body of water, the water will freeze from the top down. As ice crystals form, impurities and air bubbles are forced downward. In an ice tray, those bubbles are sealed in, creating an ice cube that's clear on top and cloudy toward the middle.

That appearance doesn't match a cocktail's aesthetic. It's inconsistent and uncontrollable, and it makes the ice melt too quickly. There are solutions, if you're willing to dive into the wonky world of clear-ice aficionados.

Ice age

"Exactly when and where ice first hit glass is impossible to say," writes New York Times critic William Grimes in *Straight Up or On the Rocks: The Story of the American Cocktail*. Ice was certainly used in some early drink preparations, but a turning point came in the 1830s with the invention of the ice plow. The plow allowed bulk ice to be harvested from lakes and ponds, and led to commercial availability of ice. (Manufacturing "edible" ice on a grand scale took till the 1930s.)

WMD

In his James Beard Award–winning *Imbibe! From Absinthe Cocktail to Whiskey Smash*, David Wondrich writes that in the 1830s, "ordinary people started getting used to the stuff, expecting it, calling for it in their drinks. Suddenly the bartending game was entirely transformed." By 1862, when Jerry Thomas published the first American cocktail guide, *How to Mix Drinks, or The Bon Vivant's Companion*, "his book and all its imitators called for ice in all forms," Grimes writes. Cobblers, swings, swizzles, and more entered the scene — a whole world of drinks with funny names that were tossed and shaken and served over ice.

VQF

DHM

The tools of the bartender's trade evolved accordingly. Cocktail shakers came on to the scene as early as the 1840s, Wondrich writes. Straws made an appearance, important for preventing ice cubes from clinking against teeth pitted by 19th-century oral hygiene. Julep strainers were another concession to old-timey tooth decay: essentially a slotted spoon that fit to the lid of a drinking glass, they were reportedly designed to keep the ice in a julep from coming into contact with the drinker's teeth.

On the bartop at Riffle, a Portland bar widely acknowledged to have the best "ice program" in town, bar manager Brandon Josie has one of the most esoteric ice-related tools: an honest-to-god swizzle stick. No, not one of the plastic novelty things most frequently seen adorned with tiny testicles at bachelorette parties, but a branch of the *Quararibea turbinata*, or "swizzlestick tree," a tree native to the Caribbean.

Strictly speaking, a swizzle stick is a long, thin branch with tiny spokes radiating out from one end. Ingredients are placed in a glass along with crushed ice, and the drink is "swizzled" by placing the spiky end in the glass and rolling the stick rapidly between the palms, like trying to start a fire in Girl Scouts.

The drink is sufficiently mixed when the glass is so cold it develops a layer of frost on the outside — an old-timey piece of cocktail lore that's being revisited in serious cocktail bars across the country.

This distinctly low-tech trick is increasingly being complemented by a very high-tech alternative: absolutely clear ice.

Crystal clear

The aforementioned air bubbles can be eliminated in high-end ice machines: Water is kept in circulation as it freezes, to prevent impurities from freezing into the ice block. The result is clear, flaw-free ice. A perfectly translucent ice cube looks prettier than a cloudy one, but there's more to it than that. The lack of air bubbles and fissures within it makes pure ice denser, which in turns lets it melt more slowly. This allows bartenders to more precisely control how their mixed drinks "age" during the time they are drunk. A single large, clear cube will melt much more slowly than a handful of standard ice cubes — a better bet if you've got a shot of nice whiskey you don't want to water down too fast.

At Riffle, Brandon Josie wrangles his ice from a Clinebell, a customized, top-of-the-line machine that produces 300-pound blocks of ice. Staffers chainsaw giant blocks into more manageable hunks, which Josie then hand-carves into cubes and tall spears.

The Teardrop Lounge's bar ice comes from a Kold-Draft machine, which freezes ice in individual "cells," producing clear one-inch cubes. The cubes are perfectly uniform, and the bar's top-notch bartenders are well versed in how long to shake a drink and how vigorously to stir, when to crack an ice cube, and when to serve it whole in the middle of a drink to slowly melt. "As geeky as we get," Sean says, "the drinks still have to be beautiful and delicious."

Most of us don't have the cash to shell out for a custom ice cube machine, but that doesn't mean the ice plutocrats and their $15,000 Clinebells have a monopoly on the clear stuff.

Google "clear ice" for a minute, and Camper English's name pops up. A San Francisco-based cocktail columnist who maintains the popular Web site Alcademics, he's written extensively about how to make clear ice in the home without the benefit of a super-spendy ice machine.

"I had heard a lot of rumors and hearsay about how to make clear ice," English says. "A lot of it sounded like a lot of hooey, to be honest. Things like 'use boiling water to make ice, leave the ice out until it turns into water, and then freeze it again.' That was one of the things that I replicated at home, and I would do the same thing like 13 times, take a picture of the ice at each round, and it showed that the ice wasn't getting clearer each time. I decided to take a more scientific approach to the problem, and confirm or deny all of the rumors about how to make clear ice. And I then ended up developing a method of doing it."

In trying to make clear ice, English "realized something really obvious about how ice freezes." After making ice in containers of various sizes, he noticed that regardless of the shape of the container, the cloudiness in any piece of ice was always in the center. He explains, "That lit the light bulb that the direction that ice freezes is important, and if one could control the direction that ice freezes, one could make clear ice wherever you want it."

English used that insight to develop an approach appropriate for the home. "My method is just to fill up an insulated cooler with regular water and let it freeze with the top off — that way ice is only forming from the top of the cooler toward the bottom, and the last part to freeze is where any trapped air or impurities are, so the first 75 percent or so of your ice will be beautiful and clear." He then chops off the cloudy portion at the bottom, and is left with a large, clear chunk of ice he can break down into cubes.

"It makes it more beautiful, and that's a huge part of what makes us like drinks," English says, explaining his fascination with ice. It's true "whether it's crazy tiki garnishes or a nice big fat clear ice cube in the bottom of the whiskey glass."

Global cooling

While some factions of the cocktail world look to the past for inspiration — viewing good ice as just one of the ingredients that bartenders once took for granted —

others are experimenting with less traditional ways of using the ingredient.

The Aviary, a Chicago bar, is widely recognized as one of the country's most innovative cocktail bars, boasting from 25 to 35 different kinds of ice. The Aviary served for a time a variation on an Old Fashioned in which booze was sealed inside a hollow sphere of ice. The lucky sipper was presented with a tiny slingshot to crack open their sphere and spill out the drink.

Riffle's Brandon Josie offers a suggestion for replicating the Aviary's drink at home: Hang a small balloon full of water in the freezer for a few hours — long enough for the outside layers of ice to freeze, but not so long that the center isn't still liquid. (It's important that the balloon hang in the freezer so that cold air can circulate around it, freezing it uniformly.) Remove the ice from the balloon, and use a screwdriver or metal pick to make a hole in the ice to drain out the liquid from the core. A syringe can then be used to fill the sphere with your booze of choice. Throw it back in the freezer for long enough for the hole to seal back up, and you've got a homemade version of one of the fanciest drinks around.

Ice's more novel formations are usually found only in cocktails, but the Whiskey Soda Lounge, a popular Thai joint with outposts in Portland and New York, sells a drink called "jelly beer," which is a sneaky way of saying "beer Slurpee." A bottle of Singha is plunged into a barrel full of ice, rock salt, and water, and rapidly jostled at sub-zero temperatures for four to five minutes. When the bottle is opened, carbonation escapes, abruptly raising the beer's freezing point — and voilà. Your ice-cold bottle of beer is transformed into a beer Slurpee. The 22-ounce bottles are served with a straw, though presumably this is more a concession to the difficulty of pouring the beer slushie from the bottle than an accommodation to modern dental hygiene.

By far the best crazy-ice experience, though, belongs to Camper English. With the help of a friend with connections to the tourism board in Newfoundland, English enlisted a fisherman to chop off a chunk of iceberg and ship it to him. "We had it stored in a special freezing room, and we all drank some delicious rum over 10,000-year-old iceberg ice," English told me. "Iceberg ice is really compressed from all the snow and ice on top of it, so there's a lot of air in there. When you pour liquid over it, the air pops like Rice Krispies. It was so ridiculous. It was spectacular."

The Wet Shave

A relaxing, rewarding, and self-indulgent morning routine.

By LEX FRIEDMAN

♦♦♦

Appeared in
Issue 2,
Oct. 25, 2013

KRX

used to hate shaving. I ranked it below flossing on my list of bathroom-related activities that I would dread. Of course, no one knew if I skipped flossing; everyone could tell if I skipped a shave.

My father taught me to shave using an electric Norelco razor, an approach I stuck with for years. My biggest problem with the Norelco electric razor was that it left me with a crappy shave. It was quick enough, but I never looked truly clean-shaven.

In college, a friend introduced me to acoustic shaving, with more-traditional, disposable razors. Over the years, I kept up with the blade arms race, switching to razors with two then three and four and even five blades over time, some with batteries that made them vibrate, some with lubricating strips, some with built-in trimmers on the flip side.

Truck drivers shaving at truck service station, Washington, DC, 1940. **Photo by Jack Delano**

I didn't like the disposable razors much either, but I stuck with them for years. The shaves were still mediocre at best, shaving the mustache region never felt great, and I found over time that blades were produced with lower quality: I'd need to chuck newer replacement blades ever more quickly.

Finally, I got fed up with shaves and razors of frustrating quality, and I made a change. It's a change that saves me money, gets me a dramatically better shave, and converted me from a begrudging shaver who hated the morning shave into a guy who looks forward to it as a highlight of the morning ritual.

Be nice and clean

Traditional wet shaving is perhaps most easily defined as "the kind of shaving your grandfather probably did." It involves the use of a safety razor, a shaving brush, shaving soap, and a handful of other supplies.

The safety razor is the most intimidating part of the setup. I use a double-edged safety razor. That's a razor that takes disposable double-edged blades. The razor itself may be the most expensive manual razor you'll ever buy; I use the Merkur Model 180 long-handled safety razor, which costs about $35.

There are many manufacturers of double-edged blades; you'll likely spend 10 cents a blade or thereabouts. Some folks change their blades once a week, while others swap them every couple of days. I use a blade for six shaves before I get rid of it.

That means I go through about 61 blades a year, or about $6.

Before you ever let one of these scary-looking blades near your face, you must first prep your face. That's where the brush and soap come into play. The brush is most commonly a badger-hair brush, though horsehair, boar-hair, hybrid, and synthetic brush options are all available (badgers and boars are slaughtered for their meat and hair; horses merely get a haircut to provide the hair for a horsehair brush). I use a cheap Tweezerman badger-hair brush; I lust after some synthetics and hybrids.

While you can use a brush in tandem with the traditional shaving creams, gels, and foams that are sold in fluorescent aerosol cans, you shouldn't. A significant portion of the joy of wet shaving comes from the slew of skin-pampering, delightfully scented shaving soaps and creams made explicitly for this form of shaving. This is where the real fun in wet shaving comes in, and I use — and enjoy — many, many brands, scents, and types of shaving soaps. My favorites include Proraso, Taylor of Old Bond Street, and Mitchell's Wool Fat.

VFX

DHS

TXK, ZZT

Lather, rinse, repeat

The purpose of the brush and the soap is to form a good lather. Wet shaving requires a wet face; you rinse your face with hot water and then apply your lather — also made with hot water — to your face. This helps open your pores, soften your stubble, and relax your skin.

I first learned to make a good lather using a shaving bowl, which is probably a smidgen easier for beginners. I now prefer face lathering because it's barely more effort, and it leaves me with one fewer thing to clean. Whether you're using a shaving soap (fairly solid) or cream (goopy), the general process is the same: thoroughly wet your shaving brush with hot water, give it a couple of good shakes, and then rub it on your shaving supply. You need a comically small amount of shaving soap or cream to make a good lather. With a solid soap, you need a little more water to get enough onto your brush; with a cream, about a nickel-sized amount does the trick. As you experiment and shave, you quickly learn: when there's tons of shaving lather left on the brush and your face is already smooth, you're using too much cream.

Get a small amount of shaving soap or cream onto the brush, and start swirling the brush in circular motions all around your face. I generally start with a thin layer of soap around my face, and then add small bits of hot water to the tip of my brush and repeat the swirling. If your brush is too wet, the lather ends up dripping down your face in annoying rivulets that won't get you a good shave. If it's too dry, your shave will hurt. Your shaving brush should end up with peaks of lather that look a lot like the shaving cream you'd squeeze from a can. Experimentation is key.

You can always add more water to your lather. Taking water out of the lather you've spread on your face is a major challenge.

Swift strokes

Once your face is fully lathered with warm, wet soap, it's time to shave.

If it's your first shave, you'll probably be a little nervous. My advice: Get a good shave with your old method the day before. Take a hot shower. Spend an extra minute soaking your face under the hot water before you shut off the shower.

Build your lather. Scrub it onto your face, adding water and swirling more as necessary. Grab your razor, and remember the three keys to successfully maneuvering the blade on your face: angle, pressure, and patience.

You want to hold the razor against your face at approximately a 30-degree angle. That is, the handle should be at a 30-degree angle, starting from parallel to the floor. That angle — depending upon your razor and blade — should just allow the edge of the blade to reach your skin, which is what we're going for.

On the pressure side, forget everything you know about disposable-razor shaving. Disposable razors use densely packed, lousy blades; you're accustomed to pushing hard against your skin to remove your facial hair. That's not how wet shaving works.

Rather, you hold the razor gently against your skin. The weight of the razor — and trust that it will weigh considerably more than the plastic doo-hickey you bought at the supermarket — provides the oomph the blade needs to cut your hair. Instead of pressure, your method for acquiring a smooth shave is repetition.

Get a small amount of shaving soap or cream onto the brush, and start swirling the brush in circular motions all around your face.

That's where patience comes in. You'll make multiple shaving passes along your face to achieve impressive smoothness. When you're new to wet shaving, my advice is to do but a single pass, with the grain of your beard. (And remember, only shave where your face is lathered. With a disposable razor, you might shave over the same spot again and again. With a safety razor, shave where there's lather. If you miss a spot, get it on the next pass, but only after reapplying lather.)

After you get comfortable with the process, add a second pass that goes across the grain of your beard — not against it. Starting your second pass requires the same prep as your first: Again rinse your face with hot water, again build a fresh lather on your face. Your brush is already loaded with lather; you don't need to reload it with soap. Add a few drops of water to the brush and then start swirling it on your re-wet face.

When you're comfortable with the across-the-grain shaving pass — give yourself a couple of weeks — it's time to add the final pass, the against-the-grain pass. Once more you rinse your face with hot water, once more you re-lather from your still well-loaded brush. Now, after again repeating your "angle, pressure, and patience" mantra, you carefully shave against the grain of your beard.

I love that third pass. My face looks smooth before it happens; it feels smooth afterward.

After the shave

When the third pass is complete, I rinse my face with cold water, and then with an alum block. This is a fragile block of soap that you can buy online; it's a naturally occurring astringent. I wet the bar with cold water, rub it all over my face, and rinse five minutes later.

The cold water and the alum block close your pores. It can help prevent ingrown hairs and other problems. I love mine. Generally, the alum block merely feels cooling. If it burns, I know that I have a shaving problem: I'm pushing too hard, my angle's off, or the blade is dull, and I'm hurting my skin with my current shave — meaning something has to change about my process.

Finally, I apply an aftershave lotion; my preference is to choose an option that's alcohol-free.

That's it?

Building a lather, making three complete shaving passes, the brush, the alum — it's an awful lot. There are not-insignificant startup costs involved with wet shaving.

For me, though, the process is well worth it. My kids object to stubble, and they give me a kiss test many mornings to verify that my face is as smooth as it ought to be. I'm saving money by not buying multi-bladed monstrosities from Schick and Gillette.

And the whole shaving process takes me 10 to 15 minutes from start to finish. Longer than it ever took before, sure, but a far more relaxing, rewarding, and self-indulgent process than any other approach I've tried. I feel like I'm caring for my face, and my face seems to appreciate the attention.

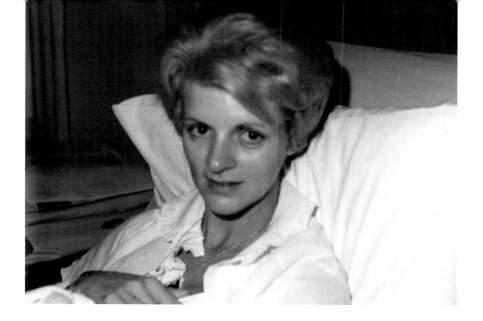

How He Met My Mother

The unlikely sequences that lead to a new life.

By JASON SNELL

Appeared in
Issue 5,
Dec. 6, 2012

'm driving my parents' car down a two-lane desert highway, my father in the passenger seat. Chauffeuring him feels a little odd, but despite his fierce independence he seems to acknowledge that it's a kindness.

From my parents' house in the Arizona outback to the suburban Phoenix hospital is an hour's drive. My father is 81. A year ago, nearly to the day, he had a pretty severe heart attack. He doesn't have much energy to begin with, and what little he had this morning he depleted at my mother's bedside.

My dad has always been a storyteller. My mother would retreat from a room as he regaled the guests with a favorite anecdote — entirely new to the appreciative crowd, but one she had heard dozens of times before. These days, his short-term memory in disrepair, he repeats those oft-told stories even more than he already did.

The author's mother at his birth. **Photos courtesy of the author and his family**

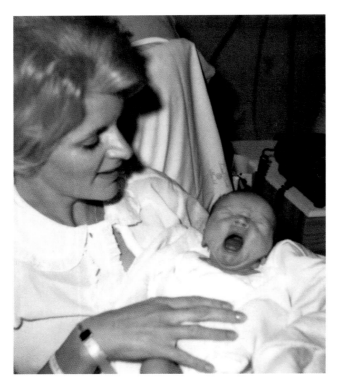

The car stereo is off for the entire drive. A child of the pre-rock era, my father has no interest in the music on my iPhone. And I'm not interested in listening to his preferred political talk-radio programs just a few days before a presidential election.

So instead, he tells me stories. And to my amazement, after knowing him for 42 years, he tells me one I haven't heard before.

Half Moon Bay

It's 1963, just months before Kennedy will be assassinated, and the man who will one day be my father has finished a long shift at the Victor Equipment Company on Folsom Street in the grungy, industrial South of Market area that four decades later will host gleaming conferences put on by Macworld, Apple, Oracle, and many other companies not yet founded.

The neighborhood will change a lot, but the weather won't. It's July in San Francisco, which generally means cold fog, but not today. Today, it's sunny and warm. Driving south toward his house on the Peninsula, my father impulsively detours to Half Moon Bay. He's never been there, but he knows it's got a beach, and today he can have that rarest of things for a San Francisco summer: a walk on the beach with no jacket.

He parks his blue MGB and walks out on the beach. There's a blonde in her early 20s sitting on a blanket, her nose in a book.[1] The woman who will one day be my mother has come to the beach as a reprieve after several days of entertaining her parents and teenage brother, who had come from Pennsylvania to visit her and her sister.

She doesn't want to talk to this strange man — she wants to be left alone. He's persistent and apparently somehow successful, because they talk for an

SYG

LFK

The author and his mother

hour or two. But the ultimate prize eludes him: she doesn't give him her full name or her phone number, and she drives off in her Corvair. He thought they had hit it off, but in the end, it's an opportunity missed.

Family math

I had known bits of the story before. I knew that my parents had met on the beach at Half Moon Bay. And I clearly recall the moment when I was 18 that they mentioned the meeting had happened a full five years before they were married. My half brother, the youngest of the three children from my father's first marriage, was born in 1964. But if they had been married in 1968 and met five years before that...

The woman who will one day be my mother has come to the beach as a reprieve after several days of entertaining her parents and teenage brother.

In that moment, my understanding of my relationship with my older half-siblings changed completely. Before, with barely any inkling of the complexities of adult relationships, I just knew they had a different mother, and that it was awkward when they came to visit my dad and his new family.

What I hadn't understood was that my mother was the Other Woman, and that my father met her nearly a year before my half-brother was born.

Future past

My father is free to drive to Half Moon Bay and chat up a skeptical blonde reader because his wife and two daughters are spending a few weeks of their summer vacation with her parents in Southern California.

From the perspective of the far future, when the Other Woman would be his wife of 44 years, it's easier to forgive his actions. I have no doubt he was unhappy in his marriage. Was there some special spark with that blonde 24-year-old on the beach, right from the start? Or is that too much to project onto a 32-year-old father of two trying to pick someone up while his young family is safely out of reach?

Regardless, my father doesn't shrug off the conversation with the blonde girl. He'd learned that she works for county health, and that she drives a rear-engine Corvair. In those innocent days, car registrations had to be in public view, so once he finds her car by checking out public-health parking lots, he gets her name by simply looking at the steering column. He calls the health department, finds out where she works, and leaves her a message, using a fake last name so she can't look him up and discover that he's married.

Now the ball is back in her court. She can ignore him again, but he's shown his interest. She must have been interested, too, or maybe just intrigued by his persistence. In any event, the girl with the Corvair relents, and returns the call of the man with the MGB.

Prepared for the worst

My mother is the healthy one. She's eight years younger and has a statistically longer life expectancy. Women on her side of the family are extremely long-lived. My father was diagnosed with serious carotid blockages in the late 1980s and has been talking about his imminent demise for the intervening two decades. He's had four major surgeries and two month-long hospital stays.[2]

So, in a sense, I have been preparing for my father's death since 1988. My wife and I talk about what we can do to support my mother after he's gone. We always figured she'd outlive him, maybe by decades.

I think about this as we pull into my parents' driveway and unload the shopping bags from the car, and I prepare to make us some dinner. An hour away, my mother is in intensive care, recovering from her emergency triple bypass.

Decision point

Four years after meeting my mother, my father is planning his exit strategy. He and his wife are enmeshed in the professional community of Walnut Creek, a suburb at the eastern edge of the Bay Area. But he plans to open a second orthodontic practice nearly a hundred miles away in the rural Sierra Nevada foothills, a move to leave his old life behind for a new one.

His wife knows there's another woman. One night, my mother had picked up the phone at her apartment, and a woman's voice had said, "May I speak to Dr. Snell, please." My father took the phone. It was his wife. The cat was out of the bag.[3]

It's 1968, and it all still hangs in the balance. Even if his marriage is over, does he know he really wants to flee to the countryside and marry his girlfriend? She wants children. He's already fathered four and raised three. Does he want to be a parent again at nearly 40?

This is all going through his mind as he's setting up his new office, a small space built directly over a creek in downtown Sonora. He's installing the furniture and equipment himself. My mother goes off to do some shopping downtown as he installs Formica countertops using contact cement. When she returns, opening the front door creates just enough air movement to waft the contact cement's fumes over the office's gas pilot light.

There's an explosion that bows the office's windows outward and creates a fireball that engulfs my father. He crawls across the burning countertops and out the door, then drops 20 feet off a deck and into the creek below. There's enough water in the creek to put out the flames, but not enough to insulate him from smashing into the rocks and cracking his ribs.[4] He climbs out of the creek and helps put out the fire in the office.

Hours later, my mother knocks on the front door of my father's house. "Your husband is in the hospital," she says.

A moment of clarity

Forty-two years after my birth, my father tells me that this is the moment that led directly to him divorcing his wife, selling his practice, giving her the house and custody of the kids and a monthly support check, and marrying my mother. In that moment he's on fire and dropping 20 feet into a rocky creek. And he knows what he wants: he wants to marry my mother and have children — well, maybe one will be enough — and leave his old, successful, unhappy life behind. Three months later the divorce is final and my parents are married.

He's telling me this part of the story at the kitchen table in their little retirement house, while 40 miles away the woman he married, the one he's always expected would outlive him, is heavily sedated after having her ribs cracked open and three veins grafted to her heart to save her life.

Two days before, I was in San Francisco and she was going in for an angiogram to find out what was causing her chest pains. Now the two of us, husband and son, are eating breakfast by ourselves in the middle of her kitchen.

What he's telling me is the story of his true love, a story in hindsight of nearly 50 years together, no matter how messy it might have been when they were living it. What I'm hearing is the complicated chain of events that explain my existence.

Thermodynamic miracles

In the landmark comic-book series _Watchmen_, the nigh-omnipotent character Dr. Manhattan can see the entirety of space and time. To him, humans — even his longtime girlfriend, Laurie — are no more relevant than ants in an anthill.

But in this dark work of fiction, set against the backdrop of Cold War–era nuclear annihilation, there comes a surprising glimmer of light. Laurie discovers that her biological father is the man who had once attempted to rape her mother. She believes that this proves her life is a meaningless joke, but Dr. Manhattan views it as an affirmation that every human life is itself a miracle:

> _Thermodynamic miracles...events with odds against so astronomical they're effectively impossible, like oxygen spontaneously becoming gold. I long to observe such a thing. And yet, in each human coupling, a thousand million sperm vie for a single egg. Multiply those odds by countless generations, against the odds of your ancestors being alive; meeting; siring this precise son; that exact daughter..._
>
> _Until your mother loves a man she has every reason to hate, and of that union, of the thousand million children competing for fertilization, it was you, only you, that emerged. To distill so specific a form from that chaos of improbability, like turning air to gold...that is the crowning unlikelihood. The thermodynamic miracle._
>
> _But the world is so full of people, so crowded with these miracles that they become commonplace and we forget...I forget. We gaze continually at the world and it grows dull in our perceptions. Yet seen from another's vantage point, as if_

new, it may still take our breath away...For you are life, rarer than a quark and unpredictable beyond the dreams of Heisenberg; the clay in which the forces that shape all things leave their fingerprints most clearly.

It's 1963, and a man impulsively decides to go to a beach he's never been to.

It's 1967, and he's on fire, falling into a shallow creek.

It's 1970, and a baby is coming into the world.

It's 1989, and a new chain of circumstances is created when I'm introduced to the woman who will become my wife.

It's 2012, and I'm serving Thanksgiving dinner in the kitchen of my parents' house in Arizona. My children are there, both with their own stories of a series of choices my wife and I made that led to their existence. My father sits at the head of the table, turkey and mashed potatoes in front of him. And next to him, home from the hospital for three weeks and recovering from her heart surgery, is his wife, my mother.

There we sit, eating dinner. Thermodynamic miracles all.

Afterword *About two months after the Thanksgiving dinner portrayed in this essay, my father passed away. The time I spent with him in the car seems all the more special now. A year later, my mother is healthy and still living in her house in Arizona. She continues to grieve for her partner of 50 years, as does our entire family.*

---

1 My father never shied away from chatting up girls, and apparently had quite a lot of success with it. Sadly, I did not inherit that trait. Instead, I inherited my mother's propensity to stick her nose in a book.

2 He's twice had surgery on his carotids, had an abdominal aortic aneurysm that burst during surgery and led to him being in the hospital for more than a month, and most recently had a heart attack that led him to another month-long hospital stay during which the doctors determined he was just too weak for open-heart surgery.

3 My father recollects that at some point in the 1960s, AT&T started to itemize every call outside a limited local area on his home phone bill. This presumably exposed countless straying husbands and wives who called their lovers while their spouses were out.

4 In the end, the fall does more harm than the fire. My father's damage from the fireball ends up being relatively minor, thanks to the dip in the creek. He acquired just a scar up one arm from crawling over the burning countertops.

BIOGRAPHIES

*Type http://magcode.me/ plus the blue code following a name to visit the
contributor's Web site. Twitter accounts are noted as T: twittername. An * indicates
an author who appears only or additionally in the extended ebook edition.*

Steven Aquino* FNK
T: STEVENAQUINO
Steven is a freelance
technology writer. His work
has appeared in *Macworld*,
TidBITS, *The Loop* maga-
zine, and Tech.pinions. He's
co-host of the Accessible
podcast, a weekly show
about accessibility on iOS.

Caty Bartholomew WMV
T: CATYBARTHOLOMEW
Caty Bartholomew is a
Brooklyn-based illustrator
and a master of both paint
and pixels. She's also a
highly acclaimed teacher
of toy design and illustration
at Parsons and at City
College of New York.

Naftali Beder* LCC
T: NAFTALIBEDER
Naftali Beder is an illustrator
living in Astoria, New York.
His drawings have appeared
in the *New York Times*, the
Los Angeles Times, and
PLANSPONSOR among
others. His work has been
recognized by the Society
of Illustrators and American
Illustration.

Lianne Bergeron ZRH
Lianne Bergeron is a
Canadian author and
entrepreneur who lives and
works near Amsterdam
with her Dutch husband
and four kids. When she's
not teaching English, writing
articles, or working on her

books, she can be found
on the road on her bicycle
built for six.

Matt Bors RVW
T: MATTBORS
Matt Bors is a political
cartoonist, editor, and
illustrator in Portland,
Oregon. His latest book is
Life Begins At Incorporation.

Gabe Bullard BKQ
T: GBULLARD
Gabe Bullard is a journalist
and the director of news
and editorial strategy at
WFPL, the public radio
news station in Louisville,
Kentucky. He also edits
Toothpick Swords, a blog
about drinks.

Serenity Caldwell NMG
T: SETTERN
Serenity Caldwell adores
hats, and wears many.
Currently, she spends her
time geeking out on the
Incomparable and racing
around a roller derby track
under the name Artoo
Detonate. If you read a
Macworld ebook in the last
few years, there's a good
chance she edited it.

Jacqui Cheng CGH
T: EJACQUI
Jacqui Cheng is Editor
in Chief at the Wirecutter,
and Editor at Large at Ars
Technica. Jacqui's writing
has also been published
in the *Guardian*, *Wired*,
and the ebook *Unmasked*.
A former back-end Web

developer, Jacqui's other
interests include gardening,
cooking, running, urban
sustainability, human rights,
and various forms of activism.

Amy Crehore (cover) GGE
T: AMYCREHORE
Oregon artist Amy Crehore
creates fine-art paintings,
book covers, a children's
book, art ukeleles, and
more. Her illustrations have
appeared in the *Atlantic
Monthly*, *BusinessWeek*,
Esquire, *GQ*, the *New York
Times*, and many other
publications.

Dominic Flask* CCH
T: DANGERDOM
Dominic Flask is a graphic
designer and illustrator
from Wichita, Kansas, who
works hard to make the
world a beautiful and more
interesting place to live
in. He creates illustrations,
logos, posters, invitations,
infographics, Web sites,
and mobile apps.

Glenn Fleishman* HCM
T: GLENNF
Glenn Fleishman is the
editor and publisher of *The
Magazine*, hosts the podcast
The New Disruptors, and
is one of the writers of the
Economist's Babbage blog.
The father of two, Glenn
won two episodes of
Jeopardy! in 2012, and
he won't let you forget it.

Lex Friedman SRR
T: LEXFRI
Lex is an author, a senior
contributor to *Macworld*,
and a podcaster. He heads
up podcast ad sales for
the Mid Roll. Lex has three
kids and one wife. His
hobbies include writing
third-person bios for
Internet publications.

Nancy Gohring* NGO
T: NGOHRING
Nancy Gohring's work has
appeared in *Wired*, the
New York Times, the
Economist Babbage blog,
MIT Technology Review,
Computerworld, *ITworld*,
and many other publica-
tions. She started writing
about cell phones
when they were huge
and expensive.

Alison Hallett* VWR
T: ALISONHALLETT
Alison Hallett is the arts
editor of the *Portland
Mercury*, an alt weekly in
Portland, Oregon, as well as
the co-founder of Comics
Underground, a quarterly
reading series that
showcases Portland's
thriving comic book scene.

Tim Heffernan TXL
T: TIM_HEFFERNAN
Tim Heffernan attended
Deep Springs College from
1996 through 1998. After
initially studying biology, he
took a degree in economics.
Today he writes about heavy
industry and the natural

world for the *Atlantic*, *Popular Mechanics*, *Pacific Standard*, and others. He lives in New York.

Chris Higgins* PJG
T: CHRISHIGGINS

Chris Higgins writes for *Mental Floss*, *This American Life*, and the *Atlantic*. He was writing consultant for *Ecstasy of Order: The Tetris Masters*. His new book is *The Blogger Abides: A Practical Guide to Writing Well and Not Starving*.

Colleen Hubbard
T: VENIVIDIEDI

Colleen Hubbard is a San Francisco–based writer of fiction and nonfiction. Her work has appeared in *Meatpaper*, CHOW, the Billfold, and elsewhere.

Thaddeus Hunt MYN
T: THADDEUSHUNT

Thaddeus Hunt has been working in IT and Web development for the last 12 years in North Carolina. Since his childhood in New England, he's been writing and telling stories. He finished writing his first science fiction novel in April 2013.

Morgen Jahnke* ZZN
T: SPECTATRIX

For the past 10 years, Morgen Jahnke has written for the Web on a variety of topics, from taxidermy shops in Paris to introversion. She lives in San Diego and is working on her first novel.

Carren Jao* PJV
T: CCJAO

Carren Jao writes about art, architecture, and design for the *Los Angeles Times*, *Architectural Record*, and KCET, among others. She's

fascinated with connections, hidden histories, and how the ordinary becomes remarkable.

Jenn Manley Lee FCS
T: JEMALE

Jenn Manley Lee resides in Portland, Oregon, with her spouse Kip Manley and daughter Taran in a house full of books, geeks, art, cats, and music.

Erin McKean GQX
T: EMCKEAN

Erin McKean is the founder of Reverb Technologies, makers of Wordnik dictionary and the Reverb app; a blogger at A Dress A Day; and the author of four books about words (including *Totally Weird and Wonderful Words*), one novel (*The Secret Lives of Dresses*), and a fashion field guide (*The Hundred Dresses*).

Scott McNulty FDQ
T: BLANKBABY

Scott McNulty is a writer living in Philadelphia. When he isn't rolling to save versus social awkwardness, he can be found reading, participating in the award-winning geek culture podcast the Incomparable, and spending time with his lovely wife.

Manjula Martin* VFY
T: MANJULAMARTIN

Manjula Martin lives in San Francisco. Her writing appears in the *Virginia Quarterly Review* online, *Maura* magazine, *Modern Farmer*, *SF Weekly*, the Rumpus, and Post Road. She founded Who Pays Writers? and edits *Scratch* magazine.

Michelle K. Martin MKM
T: MICHELLEKMARTIN

Michelle K. Martin is a New England-based photographer who has an affinity for creating colorful and simple compositions. Specializing in food photography, she also enjoys lifestyle and portrait photography.

Philip Michaels
T: PHILIPMICHAELS

Philip Michaels is the online managing editor for *Macworld*, *TechHive*, and *PCWorld*. His work has also appeared in *The Loop* magazine, Television Without Pity, TeeVee.org, and elsewhere.

Pat Moran* GVN
T: PATMORAN252

Pat Moran is a photographer from Portland, Oregon. He is also an actor, producer, and company member at Action/Adventure Theater.

Richard Moss DGB
T: MOSSRC

Richard Moss is the content editor at Archive.vg and a freelance writer dedicated to uncovering fascinating stories related to games, technology, and history. He is crazy enough to have written an ebook on the soccer-management game *Football Manager 2012*.

Christa Mrgan
T: ANTICHRISTA

Christa designs quality audio software for Rogue Amoeba, where she also occasionally blogs. She lives in the Pacific Northwest with her husband, daughter, and cat, and is pretty smug about it. Her interests include eating kale chips and playing the banjo non-ironically.

Laura Muns PKC

Laura Muns is a freelance photographer based in Haarlem, the Netherlands, where she works mostly on documentary projects. Her work has appeared in magazines and on Web sites.

Maarten Muns
T: MAARTENMUNS

Maarten Muns is a science and technology reporter based in Haarlem, the Netherlands.

David Erik Nelson BQQ
T: SQUIDAVEO

David Erik Nelson keeps house in Ann Arbor, Michigan, with his wife, toy poodle, and two human children. His writing includes the geeky craft book *Snip, Burn, Solder, Shred*, a monthly opinion column in the *Ann Arbor Chronicle*, and short stories in magazines and anthologies.

Julio Ojeda-Zapata* GBR
T: OJEZAP

Julio Ojeda-Zapata is a long-time technology journalist and an occasional author. His latest book is *The Mobile Writer*. He lives in St. Paul, Minnesota, with his wife and son.

Cara Parks KJM
T: CARAPARKS

Cara Parks has written for the *New York Times*, *Slate*, and the *New Republic*. She is the former deputy managing editor of *Foreign Policy* magazine, and she teaches as an adjunct professor at the Columbia Graduate School of Journalism.

John Patrick Pullen LKS

T: JPPULLEN

John Patrick Pullen specializes in technology and travel, having covered everything from the world's fastest ice luge track to the toughest electronics on the market. A regular contributor to *Entrepreneur* and *Fortune*, his work has also appeared in *Boston* magazine, *Men's Journal*, *Time*, and *Wired*. He is based in Portland, Oregon.

Kevin Purdy GMF

T: KEVINPURDY

Kevin Purdy is a freelance writer who lives in Buffalo, New York. He writes for *ITworld*, *Fast Company*, and *Buffalo Spree*, among other publications. He is the author of *The Complete Android Guide* and is a former contributing editor at Lifehacker.

Joe Ray RLW

T: JOE_DINER

Award-winning food and travel writer and photographer Joe Ray's work has been featured in the *New York Times*, Agence France Presse, the *Guardian* and elsewhere. He moved to Lummi Island, Washington, to write a cookbook with James Beard-nominated chef Blaine Wetzel.

Carolyn Roberts FZF

T: THESHOOGLYPEG

Carolyn Roberts lives in Scotland and works in mental health. Her work has previously appeared in *Oh Comely* magazine and on BBC Radio Scotland. When not working or writing, she spends her days chasing after her infant daughter.

Lisa Schmeiser HBV

T: LSCHMEISER

Lisa Schmeiser fell into a newsroom by accident in the 1990s and hasn't been off deadline since. Her writing has appeared in the *Minneapolis City Pages*, the *San Francisco Chronicle*, *Slate*, Television Without Pity, *Investor's Business Daily*, *Macworld*, and *TechHive*.

Brittany Shoot* XPC

T: BRITTANYSHOOT

San Francisco-based journalist Brittany Shoot, the managing editor of *The Magazine*, writes about fascinating people and far-flung places. She is a contributing writer to *Mental Floss*, *Spirituality & Health*, and *Sojourners*, and also writes for magazines including *Time*, *Open Skies*, *Scanorama*, and *Islands*.

Mark Siegal* NXY

T: MARKSIEGAL

Mark Siegal is a tech nerd who lives near Washington, DC. His background includes science writing, book publishing, and various magic tricks with spreadsheets.

Scott Simpson KDZ

T: SCOTTSIMPSON

Scott Simpson is a writer and performer from California. He spent over a decade in the digital media business at Amazon.com and Apple, and is co-host of the comedy podcast You Look Nice Today.

John Siracusa BVF

T: SIRACUSA

John Siracusa has spent 16 years as a professional Web developer and technology writer. When he's not destroying the Ars Technica CMS with 45,000-word articles, John enjoys gaming, exercising his TiVo, writing open source software, and pining for the pizza and bagels of his childhood home of Long Island.

Jason Snell HFM

T: JSNELL

Jason Snell is editorial director at IDG Consumer & SMB, publishers of *Macworld*, *PCWorld*, and *TechHive*. Prior to that, he was editor in chief of *Macworld* for seven years. His projects outside of work include the Incomparable, an award-winning podcast about geek culture. He lives in Mill Valley, California, with his wife and two children.

Jacob Souva* MTJ

T: TWOFISH

Jacob Souva has created illustrations and performed design work for Cornell University, Cameron Moll, and Mooncake Foods in NYC. He also launched a kid's app for iOS called "Puzzld!" Jacob lives in the small, rural town of Cincinnatus, New York, with his wife and two boys.

Gina Trapani LPR

T: GINATRAPANI

Gina Trapani is the founder and CTO of ThinkUp, a social-network insights engine. She is happily gay-married, co-mom to her feisty little girl, and based in Brooklyn, NY.

Kellie M. Walsh LSG

T: KMWALSH

Kellie M. Walsh's work has appeared in *Creative Nonfiction*, *The Rumpus*, *PopMatters*, and on the Web sites of Fortune 500 companies, nonprofits, and a seven-piece jazz band. She also runs a tiny creative-services business with her husband. They live with an army of houseplants in the New York City area.

Olivia Warnecke MGD

T: ITSOLIVIA

Olivia Warnecke is a graphic designer and painter. Her main love is painting unusual birds, floppy dogs, curious foxes, and other fauna. She is also an avid collector of Japanese pencils, first-edition Edward Gorey and Paul Bowles tomes, dusty old graphic design annuals, and Myrna Loy paraphernalia. She lives in San Francisco.

Brianna Wu LQG

T: SPACEKATGAL

Brianna Wu is the founder of Giant Spacekat, a game development company specializing in cinematic experiences. She's worked as a politico, an illustrator, and an investigative journalist. She likes running, dance music, and racing motorcycles.

CREDITS

"A Beacon of Hope" ©2013 John Patrick Pullen. Dry Falls photo via Wikimedia. Poster and electrical chess-set courtesy of Brent Blake. Architectural drawings courtesy of Andrew Kovach.

"Clarion Call" ©2014 Kellie Walsh. Photos © Brian Adams.

"Boldly Gone" story and photos ©2013 Chris Higgins.

"Everyday Superheroes" ©2012 Serenity Caldwell. Illustration ©2012 Jacob Souva.

"Redshirts in the Coffee Shop" story and photos ©2013 Gabe Bullard.

"The Everending Story" ©2013 Kevin Purdy.

"Choose Your Character" story ©2013 Brianna Wu. Artwork ©2013 Giant Spacekat.

"Strange Game" ©2012 John Siracusa. Screen capture ©2006 thatgamecompany.

"Roll for Initiative" ©2013 Scott McNulty. Illustration ©2013 Matt Bors.

"Look Within" ©2013 Lisa Schmeiser. Photos ©2013 Michelle K. Martin. Photo iStock / mathieukor

"Just Desert" story and photos ©2013 Colleen Hubbard.

"Down from the Mountaintop" ©2013 Tim Heffernan. Illustration ©2013 Olivia Warnecke.

"Summit Cum Laude" ©2013 Christa Mrgan. Photos © Neven Mrgan.

"Hoe Down" story and photos ©2013 Cara Parks. Collinear hoe photo ©2014 Johnny's Selected Seeds. http://www.johnnyseeds.com/

"Laid Out" ©2013 Nancy Gohring. Photos ©2013 Joe Ray.

"A Bicycle Built for Six" story and photos ©2013 Lianne Bergeron.

"Three Strikes, You Shout" ©2013 Philip Michaels. Illustration ©2013 Jenn Manley Lee.

"You Are Boring" ©2012 Scott Simpson. Illustration iStock / bortonia.

"Instant Memories" ©2013 Maarten Muns. Photos ©2013 Laura Muns.

"A Ribbon Runs Through It" ©2013 Erin Mckean. Illustration ©2013 Caty Bartholomew.

"How to Make a Baby" ©2012 Gina Trapani. Illustration ©2014 Simmons Ardell.

"Light Motif" ©2013 David Erik Nelson. Pinhole photos ©2013 Justin Lundquist. Wide-angle photo ©2011 Wade Patrick Brooks. https://secure.flickr.com/photos/pattycakee/5332499728/

"Wood Stock" story and photos ©2013 Jacqui Cheng.

"The Paste-Up" ©2013 Carolyn Roberts. Illustration ©2013 Jacob Souva.

"Icecapades" ©2013 Alison Hallett. Photos ©2013 Pat Moran.

"The Wet Shave" ©2012 Lex Friedman. Library of Congress, Prints & Photographs Division, FSA/OWI Collection, LC-USF33-020641-M2.

"Tiny Furniture" ©2013 Thaddeus Hunt. Illustration ©2013 Dominic Flask.

"How He Met My Mother" ©2013 Jason Snell. Photos courtesy of the author and his family.

Cover ©2013 Amy Crehore.

IN EBOOK ONLY

"Head Games" ©2013 Carren Jao. Photo ©2013 Eric Holsinger. https://secure.flickr.com/photos/ericholsinger/8894288151/

"Inkheart" ©2013 Nancy Gohring. Photos ©2013 Glenn Fleishman.

"Carriage Return" story and photos ©2013 Richard Moss.

"Mechanically Attached" ©2013 Morgen Jahnke. Illustration ©2013 Naftali Beder.

"Re-Enabled" ©2013 Steven Aquino.

"What Lies Beneath" ©2013 Alison Hallett. Photos ©2013 Pat Moran.

"Pinball Wizards" ©2013 Brittany Shoot. Photo ©2009 Angie Garrett. http://www.flickr.com/photos/79908182@N00/3521904252/

"Sink Your Teeth In" ©2013 Julio Ojeda-Zapata. Kryssia Campos / Flickr Open / Getty Images.

"Flaws and All" story and photos ©2013 Manjula Martin.

"Code Dependency" ©2013 Mark Siegal. "Antipodes" Photo ©2008 cliff1066. https://secure.flickr.com/photos/28567825@N03/2867244806/

"Playing to Lose" story and photos ©2013 Chris Higgins.

"The Sound of Silence" story and photos ©2012 Glenn Fleishman. Packard Campus photo courtesy of Architect of the Capitol.

This book was designed by Simmons Ardell in South Portland, Maine, using primarily Lyon Text and Avenir Next. It was printed by Worzalla in Stevens Point, Wisconsin, on 80 lb. Utopia 2. An edition of 1,500 was printed.

CONTRIBUTORS

We rely on a legion of freelance contributors with whom we have been so pleased to collaborate. We would like to thank all of those who have been part of our publication as of this book's printing.

WRITERS AND WRITER/PHOTOGRAPHERS

Adam Rothstein
Albert Wu
Alex Knight
Alex Payne
Alexandra Duncan
Alison Hallett
Amanda Giracca
Amy Westervelt
April Kilcrease
Art Allen
Ben Bajarin
Ben Brooks
Ben Greenman
Bill Lascher
Brianna Wu
Brittany Shoot
Cara Parks
Carolyn Roberts
Carren Jao
Casey Hynes
Celeste LeCompte
Chris Breen
Chris Higgins
Chris Krupiarz
Chris Stokel-Walker
Christa Mrgan
Colleen Hubbard
Dan Moren
Daniel Rutter
David Erik Nelson
Eli Sanders
Elisabeth Eaves
Elliott F. McCloud
Elly Blue
Erin McKean
Federico Viticci
Gabe Bullard

Gina Trapani
Guy English
Harry Marks
Jacqui Cheng
Jamelle Bouie
Jane Hodges
Jason Snell
Jeff Porten
Jen A. Miller
Jessica L.H. Doyle
Joe Ray
John D. Berry
John Moltz
John Patrick Pullen
John Siracusa
Jon Seff
Josh Centers
Julian Smith
Julio Ojeda-Zapata
Kellie Walsh
Kevin Purdy
Kirk McElhearn
Kyle Chayka
Leah Reich
Lex Friedman
Lianne Bergeron
Lisa Schmeiser
Lora Shinn
Maarten Muns
Manjula Martin
Marco Arment
Marco Tabini
Mark Donohoe
Mark Harris
Mark Siegal
Mary Catherine O'Connor
Matthew Amster-Burton
Matthew Latkiewicz

Michael E. Cohen
Michael Lopp
Michele Catalano
Michelle Goodman
Mohammed Taher
Morgen Jahnke
Nancy Gohring
Nate Berg
Nathan Barham
Nathan Meunier
Philip Michaels
Rich Mogull
Richard Moss
Rob Pegoraro
Robert Palmer
Rosie J. Spinks
Rusty Foster
Saba Imtiaz
Sandra Allen
Saul Hymes
Scott McNulty
Scott Simpson
Serenity Caldwell
Simon Parkin
Stefan Kamph
Stephen Hackett
Steven Aquino
Thaddeus Hunt
Tim Heffernan
Tim Maly
Watts Martin
Zakia Uddin

EDITORIAL

Alison Hallett
Lisa Gold
Nancy Gohring
Serenity Caldwell
Zachariah Cassady

ILLUSTRATORS

Amy Crehore
Andy Warner
Caty Bartholomew
Christa Mrgan
Dan Carino
Dan Perkins/
  Tom Tomorrow
Dominic Flask
Dylan Meconis
Grant Snider
Jacob Souva
Jenn Manley Lee
Mason Sklar
Matt Bors
Naftali Beder
Olivia Warnecke
Sara Pocock
Serenity Caldwell
Shannon Wheeler

PHOTOGRAPHERS

Árpád Gerecsey
Ana R. França
Glenn Austin Green
Guy deBros
Hellagraff.com
James Rooney
Joe Ray
Laura Muns
Linda Golden
Marco Arment
Matthew Morse
Michelle K. Martin
Pat Moran
Tiffany Arment